PHOTO CREDITS

Front Cover: Furman Photography

Back Cover: Ashleigh Williamson Photography

Page 111: Rebecca Kiehn Photography

Page 113: Earl Campbell Photography/Cage Fury Fighting Championship

DRIVEN

My Unlikely Journey from Classroom to Cage

CHARLIE
"The Spaniard"
BRENNEMAN

"Charlie and I go back to college wrestling days, and ever since I've known him he has been a hard-working, goal-driven person. We started working together early in his MMA career, and he used his work ethic and passion for competing to reach his goals. Charlie has always been a class act and carries himself like a professional."
Frankie Edgar
Former UFC Champion

"Ever since I've known Charlie, he's always seemed down to earth, funny, and very determined. He's a good friend of Jionni's and anytime he's at Sunday dinner, he eats more than any Italian there. I love his determination to always be the best, especially as a fighter. Nothing brings him down. It only makes him stronger."
Nicole "Snooki" LaValle
TV Personality

"Undoubtedly it's a person's upbringing and support that builds core character. Charlie had one of the finest in each regard. Parents who guided and encouraged him, and a family as well as community that provided sustained levels of assistance and approval. But the drive and accomplishment have been all his own. Charlie embodies the true nature of budding ambition and determination. Mixed with a strong curiosity to see what else is possible, he has experienced and accomplished many extraordinary things in his life. We are all very proud of him."
Louie Sheetz
Sheetz Inc.

"Charlie is someone who always leads by example. The first through the doors and the last to leave, all the while giving every ounce of himself in the pursuit of his goals. While I was teaching him about jiu-jitsu, he gave me a lesson in discipline, honesty, and integrity."

Brian McLaughlin
BJJ Black Belt, Coach
Owner, Precision Mixed Martial Arts

I have known Charlie for approximately seven years. I have been at his side for so many ups and downs that life has thrown his way, and I am most impressed at how Charlie handled both adversity and bliss. Charlie has such strong family and moral values and is highly intelligent, charming and physically gifted as an athlete. He truly is the total package—which makes it even more impressive, considering his never-ending thirst for additional knowledge and continued betterment. I am very blessed to have shared so many of life's special moments with such a great person."

Mike Constantino
Trainager (Trainer/Manager)
President, Cage Fury Fighting Championship

Charlie Brenneman is nothing short of a super hero whose mutant power is his simple unquestioning belief that he can accomplish absolutely anything he decides to. Infectious passion, unshakable determination, insatiable hunger for knowledge, and an outrageous work ethic put any task within his reach. He is the most genuinely authentic human being I know ... so much so that I'm sure he is an alien.

Justin Greskiewicz
Trainer, Professional Muay Thai Fighter
Owner, Stay Fly Muay Thai

This book is dedicated to my community and family

I've received so much support from my community over the years and so many questions about my unique career choice. This book was written to answer those questions and provide further insight into my life.

I wouldn't be the man I am today without my family. From elementary wrestling to professional fighting, you have been there by my side. I can only hope to pass on as much love to my own family.

And to Amanda. It's not easy to be my wife, yet you've supported me on my journey since the beginning. AND you've given me my greatest prize, Gracie. I love you.

In memory of Don Messing

"No Limits"

Gracias

I want to thank three people in particular for helping this book come to fruition. As much as I have to say and share with you all, I couldn't have done it without their help. Three English professionals, Keith Eldred (friend/mentor), Nicki Brenneman (sister) and Will Dickey (lifelong family friend) generously took time out of their busy lives to proofread and edit this book to help ensure I deliver a great finished product. Additionally, Keith walked me through the meticulous process of self–publishing. They share a passion for the English language and creative process, and together, we got it done!

Thank you, Keith, Nicki and Will.

FOREWORD

I have learned so many valuable lessons over the course of my career; some of them have been euphoric while others have been extremely difficult to endure. I feel an intense desire to share my story with the world and inspire people to maximize their potential in life. I hope to influence people of all ages, from young kids to adults. I have been given so much in my life, and I want to pay it forward. Whether it's in front of a camera, speaking to an audience, or simply influencing the life of my daughter, Gracie, I want to help others. The Brenneman kids are forever indebted to our parents, Butch and Marie, for everything they've given us. I am the man I am today because of the way I was raised. Though my parents might view themselves as average, they are far from it. They have raised four children to be successful, respectful adults. We love you.

FREEDOM

Every day, I sit and ponder what it is that will enable me to live the life I want to live. What type of life is that, exactly? One that allows me to have FREEDOM. Freedom means many things depending on the context. For me, the freedom I am referring to is financial and personal freedom. I am NOT looking for a way to get something from doing nothing. Working hard is a skill of mine. I get pleasure from putting in hard work and seeing it pay off. My entire current livelihood is based on working hard with absolutely no guarantee of payoff—or many times, a likely negative payoff. My perfect scenario is one that allows

I believe falling short of this dream planted in me a burning desire to succeed.

me to work hard on a daily basis, with varied skill requirements (endorsing, traveling, public speaking, teaching, writing, training, being active and encouraging others to do so), that enables me to put my head down peacefully at night knowing that I am maximizing my personal potential as a human being and providing the life I dream about for my family; one that allows my wife to stay at home and raise our child(ren) hands on, or if she prefers, pursue another of her passions. Perhaps most of all, I want a life that allows me to spread my message and the things I've learned on my journey while helping others. Why me? What have I done? Why does anyone care what Charlie "The Spaniard" Brenneman has to say?

Much of what I am is no different from the vast majority of people in this world. I come from an

My first championship feeling. I won states in 7th grade.

incredible family in a great small town in rural central Pennsylvania. I grew up in a traditional household. We all love each other. There were never any real fights between my siblings and me. My parents stressed the importance of working hard and respecting others. Grades were extremely important, as were athletics. I was a multisport athlete (wrestling, football, baseball, cross country), and I made the PIAA (Pennsylvania

Interscholastic Athletic Association) state finals twice in wrestling, finishing second both times, a blessing in disguise. I believe falling short of this childhood dream planted in me a burning desire to succeed in life. I then followed a wrestling scholarship to college and spent the next five years learning who I was and where I wanted to go ... or so I thought.

Many people go through life in a static state of comfort where there is little risk and little adventure. To be clear, I am not speaking negatively about people who choose to live life like this. However, I prefer the ups and downs of a lifestyle that challenges me every single day, and not just physically. Sometimes, when looking at my life from the outside in, which I often do, it seems as though there is more heartache than happiness. Trust me, there are many sides to this dynamic lifestyle that are less than enviable.

The mental toll is much more intense than the physical side of fighting. With enough practice and training, the physical aspect becomes second nature, instinctual. The mental aspect is something that takes getting used to, and I am still learning that to this day. When you live in a traditional lifestyle with a 9-5 job, you tend to get into a routine. Many people are able to live life relatively seamlessly, getting their work done as they should and remaining free from the constant scrutiny of others. When you live life in the public eye, however, you become a target for the good, the bad, and the ugly. There is no shelter, especially with today's technology. You couldn't hide from the scrutiny if you changed your name and moved to the North Pole. Trust me, they'd find you. I've seen both sides of the coin. I've been praised as the next great thing and condemned to a career (and life) of misery by the "fans" of MMA (mixed martial arts, the name of my sport).

THE BEGINNING

After graduating from Lock Haven University of Pennsylvania (or as you'll see it throughout the rest of this book, PA; that's how you say it when you're from PA), I took a job teaching Spanish in my hometown of Hollidaysburg. It really couldn't have happened any more smoothly. A Spanish position became vacant (my former Spanish teacher essentially waited for me to graduate until he retired), and an assistant coaching position became available in wrestling. I was coming back home to teach and coach. I'd always been a small town kid, so I had no qualms about coming back home. I had traveled all over the world during college. I had grown and evolved and just capped off a pretty good collegiate wrestling career. I knew where I wanted to be.

But when I got there, where I wanted to be, I realized, at 23 years of age, I still had a burning desire for "more"—more adventure, more ups and downs, more challenges, more successes and failures, all of it. I wasn't ready to sit back and live a normal life...yet. But I really had only one skill, aside from my intellect, and that was wrestling. How could I use wrestling to make a living? Well, some of wrestling friends from college were fighting in the UFC (Ultimate Fighting Championship, the biggest fight organization in the world) at the time and were succeeding. Although I was the furthest thing from a "fighter," I knew I could do what they were doing. In my eyes, it was a sport with a distinct set of skills. By hard work and dedication, I could master those skills and make myself a fighter.

But I really had only one skill, and that was wrestling.

In my second year of teaching, after a long day in the classroom, I remember sitting in my bedroom (I lived with my parents) talking to my college roommate on the phone. I was a fan of MMA but hadn't yet started training. We were talking about Frankie Edgar and Tim Boetsch (wrestling colleagues of ours who were finding success in the UFC), and, in an epiphany kind of moment, I said, "Dave, one day I'm going to fight in the UFC."

He responded, "I have no doubt that you will. You always do what you say you are going to do."

It was a moment I'll never forget. I had never thought of myself like that, from the outside looking in. I simply do what I do and don't give it a second thought. Dave helped me realize that I had something special, that I had a gift for setting goals and working hard to see them through. Mind you, I was a 24-year-old kid sitting on my childhood bed in my parents' house, had never fought a day in my life (aside from a scuffle at age 12), and I didn't know the first thing about the UFC or MMA. I just knew that I now had a purpose. At that moment in my life, I knew it was going to happen. There was no doubt. I would live my life in a way that would make that dream come true.

I had stayed active those first few years of teaching, even before dabbling in MMA. I ran a marathon, something I never thought I could or would ever do. But (as weird as this sounds to a non–wrestler) it was that feeling of grabbing hold of someone and throwing him down that I truly missed. The physicality of wrestling, of my life, was now gone. I had competed in wrestling for 15 years and had essentially thought about it every day of my life during that time. Then one day, college was over, and I was no longer a wrestler. Who was I then? What was my purpose? I thought the professional world would answer those questions, but I was wrong.

Check out this outfit. First day of my second year of teaching, 2005.

9

PROS VS. JOES

Looking back, if I had to pinpoint one single event, a tipping point, that led me to my future career, it was my experience on *Pros vs. Joes*, which was a new reality show that pitted amateur athletes against professionals in various athletic contests. Whichever "Joes" performed the best against the "Pros" won. Prior to *Pros vs. Joes*, I had never thought of mixed martial arts as a career. It was just something new and exciting that filled a competitive void in my life. That was all about to change, as was my future. One day after teaching, I was sifting through my mail and saw a piece of "junk" mail (I use quotes not because I think junk mail is anything more than annoying junk, but because of how valuable this piece of "junk" turned out to be). I opened the letter and saw that it was an informational flyer about a new reality show on Spike TV called *Pros vs. Joes*. The premise of the show was that amateur athletes ("Joes") would be given the chance to compete against former professional athletes ("Pros"), and whichever "Joe" performed the best would take home a $20,000 prize. The application deadline had already passed, but I shot them an email stating every reason why I should be on the show. I had no idea what I was getting into. I wrote what I thought they wanted to hear, though I didn't even know who "they" were. I tried to sound as respectfully cocky as I could. After all, this was TV—they like that, right?

A few weeks passed, and I got a response email stating that I had been selected to submit further application materials. My excitement turned to "Oh man!" when I saw how thorough the next few rounds of the application process were.

We, meaning my good friend and future media guy, Matt Anderson, and I got to work. At the time, Matt was working at Sheetz, a local place of awesomeness far exceeding its category of "convenience store chain," and we were always looking for something to do after work. We made an application video in one day. Because I succeeded at several sports growing up, it's assumed I'm a natural athlete, which, to some degree, I am. However, when I did the 100-yard sprint for the application video, Matt seriously had to ask me if I had run so slowly on purpose as a sort of gag. Not the case—I sprinted. HARD. Anyway, we sent the video overnight and waited to hear back yet again. And we did hear back. Over the next few months, I would go back and forth with the producers of *Pros vs. Joes*. This was a national TV show, and the entire process was extremely thorough. Aside from the video, I had to complete two application booklets, 20 pages each, covering nearly every aspect of my life, as well as a background check. It was intense. If you've never been involved with reality TV, you basically—no, actually—sign your life away. But whatever, I wanted to be on TV. (I say that jokingly, but thank God it all worked out well). When I finally got the phone call that I had been selected to compete on *Pros vs. Joes*, I was ecstatic, but my devil's-advocate self started to doubt the whole process. This was prior to the "catfish" phenomenon on the Internet (pretending to be someone/thing online that you really aren't), but still, I was just a normal kid from a normal small town—naïve to say the least. That doubt came to an end when the trip itinerary showed up in my inbox.

If you've never been involved with reality TV ... you basically sign your life away.

I was on my way to California, but they made it very clear that what happened in California stayed in California. I have a natural fear of authority, so my lips were sealed. I still remember the drive home from the Pittsburgh airport after I filmed the show. My family approached me with, "Well???" I responded, "Well what?" I stayed tight-lipped. (Maybe.)

As I stated earlier, I was still an active person when compared to the general public at this time, but nothing like what I had been in college. I could've gone into *Pros vs. Joes* as a "pretty in-shape" guy, but instead I treated it like a big wrestling tournament. I got to work—track workouts, agility training, early-morning treadmill workouts at the high school. This was my chance to break free of the standard mold, and I was determined to do so. An opportunity had been placed in my lap, and I was going to do every last thing in my power to take advantage of it.

Arriving in California, my eyes were wide open. I had traveled a good bit in college, but I'd never been to California, nor had I been exposed this up close and personal to professional athletes. What a shift my life was about to take. I wasn't necessarily in total awe of the situation, but I was in total admiration. I was given the chance to be around some of the best athletes in the world— Major League Baseball catcher Darren Daulton; NFL running back Hershel Walker; NBA stars Clyde Drexler, Dominique Wilson and Xavier McDaniel; Major League pitcher John Rocker; World Cup Soccer champion Brandi Chastain; Olympic sprinting champion Justin Gatlin; NFL and professional wrestling superstar Bill Goldberg; as well as Steelers linebacker Kevin Greene. All of these athletes were very cordial and made the experience even more memorable. Being from Central PA and a Steelers fan from birth, it was extra-special meeting Kevin Greene. Clyde Drexler was sort of the father-figure, very kind and considerate, making sure that we Joes were comfortable.

It's not very often you get to come face-to-face with superstar athletes, so I wanted to make my time

I wasn't in total awe, but I was in total admiration.

worth it, both for TV purposes AND for the sake of telling my friends all about it. In a not-well-thought-out plan, I decided to talk a bit of crap to Goldberg during the show's introduction. I let him know how lucky he was that we didn't have to wrestle. Goldberg is a big dude to say the least. His fingers are the size of hot dogs, and his fist covers my entire face. As soon as I got my little comment out, he served me up on a platter and cut me right back down to size, all while the cameras were rolling. I was legitimately scared. We were about to play football, and he was a big guy who could inflict some serious damage upon me. After the segment, I immediately found him and apologized. He responded something like, "It's okay, kid, it was just for TV." Thank you, TV!

A changing point in my life, a thing that would drive me to mixed martial arts and ultimately the UFC, came during the preparation and execution of *Pros vs. Joes*. Prior to leaving for California, I began to feel a peace of mind in relation to the upcoming competition. This was a new sensation. In my previous competitive days, I had always dealt with self-doubt in one form or another. In wrestling, for as long as I can remember, I had always doubted myself and my abilities. Granted, I was a very confident athlete, but at the most vital times, self-doubt would creep into my head. "Who am I to win?" "I'm just Charlie Brenneman." "He's wearing the new Dan Gable wrestling shoes; he must be tough." You name it, I worried about it. I was often controlled by the self-fulfilling prophecy (If you think you'll win, you will. If you think you'll lose, you will). Granted, the self-fulfilling prophecy is not set in stone, but the absolute truth is that your mental game directly affects your physical game.

Later in life, I would come to understand the power of positive thought and how it can directly affect the outcome of any situation. (You'll hear more about that.) Well, finally, at age 24, I had taken control of my mind. When I arrived in California, I was there to do one thing: WIN. I was going to collect my $20,000 prize and go home. There was zero doubt. I hadn't yet met my opposition, but it didn't matter. I was put in this situation to win. Period.

And win I did. I performed when the pressure was on. I took control of my emotions. We raced in the 100/200 meter sprint, played "one yard line" with Kevin Greene and Goldberg, wrestled John Rocker off the mound, and even tried to tackle Hershel Walker (emphasis on tried). When all of the scores and times were tallied, I was the victor, just as I had envisioned.

The $20,000 prize would fit nicely into my bank account as I resumed my normal day-to-day activities back in the classroom. But not long after victory, I received a phone call from the producers of *Pros vs. Joes*. There was going to be a finale episode, and I had a spot on the show if I wanted it. Additionally, I was able to select a partner to come with me. The finale would pit three teams of two Joes against a team of two Pros. Who was I going to take with me? Best friend? One of my brothers? There was definitely a sense of obligation in the selection process, but at the same time, I wanted to win the competition. We were playing for a brand new 2007 Dodge Caliber, and my 1997 Civic was just not cutting it any more! I really only had three choices—my best friend Dominick, or one of my two brothers, Ben or Scott. After some internal debating, I finally decided on Ben, and that decision would begin to forge the relationship that exists today between my brother and me. It wouldn't be right if I didn't mention how helpful and accommodating my administration at the Hollidaysburg Area School District was at this time. Without their cooperation, I wouldn't have been able to be on the show in the first place. I learned a great deal from my administration on how to lead. I guess they saw the bigger picture in all of this.

Ben and I took home the grand prize and were crowned champions of Season 1, *Pros vs. Joes*. It was a neck and neck race that went down to the wire. As time was ticking away, I was able to sneak past Kevin Greene and cross the goal line for a score, which enabled us to finish seconds faster than our counterparts. As I shouted at the camera, we were the "Pros of the Joes!" We each received a brand new 2007 Dodge Caliber. A small, but defining, event occurred here which would foreshadow Ben's skills as my future Chief Advisor. I was so thrilled at the thought of getting a new car that I wasn't too picky with the specs. Any car would have been fine—at the time, I was driving a not-so-mint-condition Honda Civic. But Ben, as I would soon come to realize, and later in life have come to appreciate, was a stickler for detail. It took a

That decision would begin to forge the relationship that exists today between my brother and me.

month or so before we heard anything about how we would actually get the car. The show would contact a local dealer, and, from there, we'd pick up the cars. Once all the details were worked out, and we got a rundown of what we were actually getting, Ben noticed some discrepancies. Namely, the Calibers we were receiving didn't have a sunroof. Ben quickly pointed out that the car on the show had a sunroof, and since we won that exact car, we should get a sunroof. After a bit of back and forth with the producers, we got the sunroofs we were promised, no problem. (Ben also noted that we were also entitled to chrome wheels just like the car on the show had, but I convinced him to not push our luck). In business, small details can change the dynamics of any transaction. Fortunately for me, Ben had/has a natural knack for the small details.

GETTING INTO MMA

When I decided to dabble in MMA, I did what made sense: I found the best gym in my area. I hit the road. I made the 40-minute commute to Cambria Martial Arts Academy to get the best training I could, and I also trained at a few local gyms. Little did I know at the time how much of my life would be spent on the road in search of the best training I could find. Day in and day out, I was training to be a fighter, and a few months later, I started my amateur career. I'll never forget my first amateur fight. We got into a van, drove to Steubenville, Ohio and set our sights on Next Level Fights.

Boy, were we introduced to mixed martial arts! It was the classic dark, dank venue with a sort of amphitheater feel to it. Steubenville is just past Pittsburgh and into Ohio, and to say it's a hard town would be accurate. The sport was still relatively new at this point, and now we were along for the ride. A few members of my family and a few friends packed into a 16-passenger van and headed into no man's land. To say we were out of place would be an understatement. Our entire group was about as into fighting as a camel is into snow. But at that point, I started to realize a very valuable lesson: We are what we do. From that day forward, I was a fighter. There was nothing that could stop me from believing that.

BIRTH OF "THE SPANIARD"

"The Spaniard." Where exactly did the name come from? There is a definite story, but depending on where and when you ask me, you might get the condensed version. A lot of people assume the moniker came from the movie Gladiator, as Russel Crowe's character, Maximus, goes by the nickname "Spaniard." Well, prior to my MMA journey, as stated earlier, I was a Spanish teacher. An interest in Spanish was instilled in me at a young age. When I was in eighth grade, my family hosted an exchange student from Mallorca, Spain. Luis was with us for an entire school year. Never before had I seen, firsthand, the fascinating world of other languages and cultures. When Luis came to us, he didn't speak a word of English; when he left, he was fluent. It blew me away. At a young age, I took a strong interest in the Spanish language and culture. Fast-forward a few years, and the evolution of "The Spaniard" begins. Every summer during college, we (the Lock Haven wrestling team) would help run camps all over the Northeast. Our coach, Rocky Bonomo, and his twin brother, Rick, would host these events and bring some guys from the team along to help. They are two of the funniest people I've ever met; I often say Rock, who was my coach, is one of my top five favorite people (no offense, Rick!). Rocky was a two-time All-American, and Rick was a three-time Division I national champion at Bloomsburg University. These two bounce off each other in sync, and their stories go on for days. One of the classics is how Rick was all bent out of shape prior to his third national championship match. He just couldn't figure out which way he was going to signal the number "3" to the crowd after he won his third title. At such a pivotal point in one's wrestling career, you would naturally expect far deeper and more serious concentration. But Rick just couldn't decide which three fingers he would wave in the air; he didn't think twice about the stage he was on. That's the kind of guy he is, great and hilarious.

In their younger days they would host the "Rick and Rock Show" at the conclusion of each camp, performing acrobatics, slow-motion moves, and even tossing kids high in the air (this was prior to the insane liability-filled world we now live in). As Rick and Rock carried a fun, comical theme throughout their camps, they would assign each of us a nickname. Many times, it stuck camp after camp, year after year. In the beginning, I was referred to as "Antonio Banderas" (the famous Spanish actor). At the time, I had very long, curly hair, resembling Antonio's, and I was on my way to becoming a Spanish teacher. As "Antonio Banderas"

For my first amateur fight, I gave myself my own nickname. I was "The Machine."

wasn't the toughest sounding name on the wrestling mat, it eventually morphed into "The Spaniard." Many kids would go through camp not knowing my real name. Once I began fighting, the search for a nickname began, kind of. I didn't want to be one of those people who gives himself his own nickname, but rather develop one organically. Well, for my first amateur fight, I did give myself my own nickname. I was "The Machine." It didn't stick, and the only other nickname I'd ever had was "Dirt." (I had a bad habit of getting extremely dirty as a kid, so my Godfather referred to me as "Dirt." Twenty-five years later, he still does). The name is great, but it doesn't fit into fighting. It was (next to) a no-brainer—"The Spaniard" was born. Though the name doesn't come from Gladiator, we have taken a part of that movie and

Behold
"The Machine."

22

implemented it in my career. I can remember many fights, in between rounds or in the middle of the fight, hearing my fans chanting, as in the movie, "Spannnniard, Spannnniard, Spannnniard."

DAVE AND DARCY

Through one of my old training partners, I was introduced to Dave and Darcy Regala. They are a set of identical twin corrections officers "up the mountain" (local lingo to explain that they lived, well, up the mountain—Cresson Mountain), and two of the most giving, helpful people I have ever met. They run Cambria Martial Arts Academy (CMAA), located in South Fork, PA. CMAA is a 40-minute drive from my parent's house, and I would make that trip several days a week after teaching. Winters "up the mountain" are rough, so many of those trips were spent squinting through the snowfall and sliding all over the place. I guess I was a natural in wrestling, but stand-up fighting was another thing. I can clearly remember how unimpressed the two brothers initially were with me. They knew I was a good wrestler, so their hopes were high, but their hopes were diminished quite a bit when they saw me throw my first kick. It makes me laugh even today. Despite my awful kicking technique, I was a blue chip prospect in their eyes. I had a solid wrestling background, and from the outset, they could tell I was a hard worker and would do what they told me. However, when I threw that first kick, I looked like a fish out of water, and not just any fish—a pathetic fish. Years later, Darcy would joke about how bad I looked that first day, and how much work we had cut out for ourselves. We formed a close bond, and the two brothers spent countless hours with me. They never asked for a dime. Either they would drive down the mountain, or I would drive up to them. When I would make my trips back home to PA over the years, Dave and Darcy were always up for training. We'd meet wherever we could find an open space and get to work. There was often a

Throughout life, you'll meet a precious few people who are genuinely interested in helping you, with no expectations in return.

fighter or two from CMAA who would come with them to spar, and, whether the room was 40 degrees or 100 degrees, we always got it in. Throughout life, if you're lucky, you'll meet a precious few people who are really, genuinely interested in helping you, with no expectations in return. Be it in business, sport, whatever it may be. Well, the Regalas are two of those people. For them, the intrinsic value of what we were doing, the work we were putting in, and the journey we were taking were worth it. We started out in Hollidaysburg and South Fork, PA. We fought all over the Northeast, and even down in Fort Hood, Texas for a UFC fight. I can never pay them back for what they did for me, financially or otherwise—I can only pass it on to the next kid looking to make his mark. I've always tried to show my gratitude for what they've done for me, and I hope they realize how much it means.

My first MMA championship belt, 2007. A milestone that kept me moving ahead. The Regala Twins could not have been more generous to me. Darcy is to my right, Dave to my left. (I think.)

ADIOS SEÑOR!

Before long, I had made up my mind that I wanted to leave the security of my hometown and full-time Spanish teaching job to pursue fighting. This was by no means an easy decision. I had ALWAYS done the "normal" thing. In the twenty-sixth year of my life, I was deciding to go against the grain. Step one was explaining this crazy idea to my family. As I had said, we are a very close family, and not just immediate family, either—aunts, uncles, cousins, grandparents—we're all close. There is a running joke in our family that whatever you tell one Grassi sister (my mom and her two sisters), you tell all Grassi sisters. (Except it's not a joke.) As a transition to my new career, with the extra encouragement of my mom, I decided to go back to school and earn a master's degree in the interim. She basically said, "If you're going to quit your job, you're getting a master's."

I knew enough to say OK. My parents were surprisingly very supportive of my decision—not that they didn't always support my siblings and me, but this situation was a bit different.

I was accepted into a Graduate Assistant Program at East Stroudsburg University in Eastern PA and started to coach wrestling. I left the professional world and became a student once again. For a few reasons, the transition was surprisingly tough. First, I had once thought my days of research papers and lectures were over, so that took some getting used to again. A second issue I didn't expect was the relationship between professor and student. I had been on the professor end of it for several years, so it took some readjusting to transform back into the student. I was in mixed classes of undergraduates and graduates, and I found it difficult that a few professors slotted me into the stereotype of "young college kid who doesn't know about life yet." Granted, I only had three years of experience, but I was still a professional. Eventually, I just stayed the course and got through it. Coaching helped ease some of the stress, as I had a great relationship with the head coach, Joey Rivera, and the guys on the team. ESU served an important role in my development and was a great fit at the right time in my life. I came away from East Stroudsburg with some great memories and lifelong relationships, including Laurie (who opened her home to me) and Maryanne and Joe (two of my most loyal fans, who became my great friends.)

AMANDA

"Behind every great man is a great woman," and my great woman's name is Amanda, my wife (and of course you, Mom). I am lucky that she didn't tell me to hit the bricks many years ago as I was "figuring out" what I wanted in life. I had grown up in a very conservative way, living in a small town and then going to college in another small town. However, once I started traveling and seeing the world, my mind started to open up. I was a typical young adult with crazy dreams and fantasies. I saw lifetime commitment as an end, not a beginning. I live a pretty structured lifestyle, so whether I was single or married didn't really affect anything. But back then, you couldn't tell me any differently. I wanted to live my life "freely" and come and go as I wished. I was young. I thought too much. I realize now that I didn't know what I was thinking. For several years following college, Amanda and I played the long-distance relationship game. A semester after I left LHU, Amanda returned to Middletown, PA to become a teacher, too. We would see each other nearly every weekend. Life on the road was nothing new, but we sure didn't know that it would continue for another ten years, and even longer for me. There was no real end in sight. We were both comfortably employed in our hometowns, surrounded by our friends and family. One way or another, we were going to make it happen. And then, right when I was settled into my future, I decided to change the course of my life.

When I decided to leave my job to pursue a professional fighting career, everything I knew was about to change. I was changing as a person. Not for better or worse, I just had new ambitions and philosophies. I had never really gone against the grain. I lived life safely. But now, at age 26, I was stepping out on a limb. This time period was not one of the brightest spots in my relationship with Amanda. To be honest, I was in a stage of my life where I wanted total freedom. I was selfish. I didn't want to answer to anyone. I wasn't a bad person; I just wasn't quite mature enough to give a part of myself to someone else. I wasn't ready. Simply put, I was young and afraid of marriage.

While in graduate school, I went to class and socialized a bit, but my life was dedicated to getting my master's degree, coaching wrestling and training as a professional fighter. An unfortunate cost of this new "freedom" was my relationship with Amanda. My head was like aluminum in a microwave. Thoughts were bouncing around my cranium at warp speed in every direction. I wanted space, and Amanda was a master at giving me exactly what I wanted. I went through what is one of the least-proud stages of my life. The "I don't know what I want, and I don't know why" stage. Amanda played me like a drum. Well done, Love. She stopped picking up calls and responding to texts. I was yesterday's news to her. And of course, the more we were apart, the more I wanted to be with her. She was a pro, and it worked. I was entering my late twenties, and my philosophies of life were evolving. I began to realize that I wanted marriage and children, and these always came back to her. It meant more to me to be with her than to have the freedom to move to Spain or move out west for training

She played me like a drum.

or whatever other crazy impulsive thoughts I had. Up to that point, I had been living my life for things that might or might not have been, not for what was.

Thankfully, after a buffing-out period, Amanda and her family welcomed me back into their lives. They made me earn it, though. Amanda's parents are two of the nicest, most gentle people in the world. But that first time I walked back into their house, her mom burned a hole right through me with that glare. I knew enough to never cross them again.

TRAINING IN EASTERN PA

After I relocated to Eastern PA, I did what I did back home: I found the best gym around. Unfortunately, the gym was in Philadelphia, a two-hour trip from East Stroudsburg. Many nights, I would drive two hours, train for two hours, and then turn around to drive two hours home. Fight Factory was a prominent gym in Philadelphia, and this was my first real taste of a high-level fight gym. They welcomed me with open arms. A few years earlier at a seminar near home, I had met one of their best fighters, Eddie Alvarez, and we clicked. He helped introduce me to everyone at Fight Factory, and I couldn't have asked for a better group of guys. A few of them are still involved in my career today.

Around this time, I was also introduced to expenses such as gas and toll money—and boy do they add up, especially when you're living on a graduate assistant's salary. Granted, I had saved a good bit from my three years of teaching, as well as from *Pros vs. Joes*, but that's just it, I saved it. I didn't want to run right through it. For the next year or so, I made the trek over to Philly once or twice a week, and I also reconnected with college wrestling friend and rising UFC star Frankie Edgar. Frankie was well into his fighting career at the time, and he was nice enough to include me in his world of training. We had been acquaintances in college, knowing each other through mutual friends, and he wasn't obligated to help me out. I'd like to think I was of some value to him—while I was able to pick his brain, I served as a nice punching bag in return. In addition to the Philly trips, I was now traveling almost two hours to New Jersey (South/Central Jersey) to train with some of the best fighters on the east coast—who would eventually become the best in the world. I was surrounding myself with the right people, the best. Many years later I would realize that this was one of the key factors in my success, something I pass on to youngsters looking to follow their dreams—surround yourself with the best.

This was one of the key factors in my success, something I pass on to youngsters looking to follow their dreams.

Another concept I learned early on in my fighting career was the importance of networking. It's not just about how good you are, it's about how good you are

AND who you know. I was networking without even knowing it. Frankie is one of the most respected people I know. By doing what I do, training hard and giving 100%, he came to respect me. Any time you have someone like him in your corner, it can only help. Frankie and Chris Liguori, another big influence on my career, took me under their wings and walked me into the world of MMA.

SHATTERED SOCKET

As Chris and Frankie were taking me under their wings, I was beginning to feel comfortable with the actual techniques of fighting. Striking is something that doesn't always come naturally to a wrestler, but after a few years of hard work, I was beginning to gain some confidence. Then, in May of 2008, while preparing for an upcoming fight, I met up with Frankie and Chris in Perth Amboy, New Jersey, for a sparring session. This would be the last hard sparring before my fight the following week, so the plan was to get this one in and

In the blink of an eye, my world was rocked.

then go through the motions until the fight. The session was going just like every other one, with the three of us rotating in and out every few minutes. The room was very warm, and I was completely soaked in sweat. Then, in the blink of an eye (no pun intended), my world was rocked. Chris had thrown a head kick, and it landed in the perfectly wrong spot. The way I explain it is like this: Chris pulled the kick (he let off power, since it was a head kick), which took some distance off the kick. That, coupled with my instinctive

I reached my hand shakily up to see if my eyeball was still inside my skull.

reaction of leaning back, caused the toe region of his foot to land right in my eye socket. Boom! I saw nothing out of my left eye. Only black. I instantly fell to my knees and whipped off my gloves. The pain was as intense as I'd ever felt before. I was hunched over in pain, agonizing, blind in one eye, when I felt a liquid squirting from my head. In a moment I'll never forget, I reached my hand shakily up to see if my eyeball was still inside my skull. It was; the blood was coming from a cut above my eye. Hunched over in pain, my entire future passed before me. How would I live the rest of my life with only one eye? I could surely never fight again.

Every random thought—from having a nice little picnic to the image of driving a car with one eye— entered into my mind at a thousand miles per hour. Chris and Frankie rushed to my side.

Later on, Chris would tell me that, although he was comforting me, telling me I'd be fine, he knew something was wrong when he saw my eye looking 90 degrees to the right. Five minutes after the accident, I started to see a little bit of light. Within a few more minutes, I could start to make out blurry shapes. I was gaining hope, but we knew something was seriously wrong.

With the help of another friend, MMA referee Kevin Mulhall, we went to the nearest hospital in Perth Amboy, NJ. They saw me into a waiting room, and Chris called my mom back in PA to let her know what had happened. I was transported to a bed, and I lay there writhing in pain for hours before any personnel were able to see me. It didn't matter how I lay or where I put pressure, there was no escaping the pain. I was still soaking wet from training, but now I was in a highly air-conditioned room at the hospital. I was shaking from pain and from being cold. After a few hours, a nurse was able to hook up a line of morphine to dull the pain. I had never experienced morphine before, and I hope to never again. I could feel it flow, and as soon as it permeated my entire body, I vomited. I'm not sure I've ever been in a worse situation.

Frankie, Chris and Kevin eventually left. They really took care of me that day and showed their true character. From Perth Amboy, I was transported to UMDNJ (University of Medicine and Dentistry of New Jersey) in Newark. I vaguely remember being told to decide between UMDNJ and a top vision hospital in Philadelphia, and I guess I chose UMDNJ. It turned out to be a great decision.

My parents arrived in Newark, and the doctor who examined me determined that I had a blowout fracture of my left orbital socket. Basically, the circle of bone surrounding my eye had been obliterated. However, I had to wait a week before I could have surgery because there was too much swelling. My vision had returned at this point, but I had double vision, something that was to go away after surgery. The next two months would see my parents and me drive across PA and New Jersey week after week for visits, surgery, checkups and, finally, clearance. It takes approximately five hours to get from Hollidaysburg to Newark, and again, my parents never batted an eye. Dr. Turbin, who performed my surgery, was awesome. This guy was top-notch. Fortunately, he had dealt with a variety of professional athletes, mostly NHL players, so he was very understanding and thorough when it came to resuming my sport. He had placed two mesh plates inside my previous socket, and over time, tissue permeated the plates to form a strong new socket. He even met up with me at a deli in New Jersey on his own time to check up on my progress. He was invested in my recovery. Dealing with double vision was nothing short of annoying. For six weeks after surgery, while everything was internally settling, I saw two of everything. Imagine one plane of sight going straight out as normal, and then another plane going downward at a 45-degree angle. Oddly enough, there were no restrictions put on my driving. I was doubly safe during that time on the road! At one point, we thought I might need another surgery because my eye wasn't gaining the mobility that Dr. Turbin thought it should have. On one visit, to test my eye's mobility, he placed a pair of forceps directly onto my eyeball to force it left and right, up and down. Ouch! In time, healing was on track, and, within a few months, I was cleared to fight.

MMA IN PA

I was making a name for myself on the east coast, mainly fighting in Atlantic City. I was 7-1 as a professional fighter at this point, and my only loss was to a fighter who had signed to the UFC immediately following our fight. Then about 2009 something big happened for the sport, and it was certainly beneficial to me. MMA was becoming more mainstream and being sanctioned in many more states across the country (a sanctioned event is a legal event run by that state's athletic commission). It became sanctioned in my home state of Pennsylvania. This. Was. Awesome. No longer did I need to travel several hours to Atlantic City, nor did my fans have to make the five-hour trek across two states to come support me. Granted, we did have some fun in Atlantic City, and, boy, did we make a statement with our royal blue

Spaniard shirts! (Top fighter Eddie Alvarez had taught me a valuable lesson at the beginning of my career. Put simply, he said, "If you don't promote yourself, no one will," i.e., create as much steam around yourself as possible). My "Spaniard" shirts would become a staple in my career, but we'll get to that later. A new chapter had begun, and what an amazing adventure I had fighting in and near my hometown of Hollidaysburg, PA. With the legalization of MMA in PA, my original trainers, Dave and Darcy, created their own promotion, Iron Will Fighting Championship, and held fights in Central PA.

My first fight back home was at the Johnstown War Memorial with thousands of my fans in attendance. It's important to note here that one of the biggest motivating factors when I set out to chase my UFC dream was to make my hometown proud. My family, friends and fans had all followed and supported me throughout my entire wrestling career. They helped me rebound after falling short of the coveted state title—twice—followed my wrestling career to LHU, and then welcomed me back with open arms as a teacher. Now, we were fresh into another journey right here in Central PA. After a few fights for Iron Will Fighting Championship in Johnstown, I had the opportunity to fight in Altoona, PA at the Jaffa Mosque (the common name for the local Jaffa Shrine Center). The Jaffa was 15 minutes from where I grew up, and it was the same Jaffa Mosque we went to as kids for the

There is a certain risk you take when fighting at home.

circus and WWF wrestling. We were right in my backyard, which was great news. However, there is a certain risk you take when fighting at home. Everyone expects you to win. Everyone expects an unbelievable performance. Winning in this environment is an unbelievable high, but losing? I don't even want to think about it.

SELLING TICKETS

The more tickets you sell to your fight, the more money you make. This is the business model for local and regional promotions. I understand the concept, but I'm not the biggest fan of the model. Yes, promoters need to make money, but fighters fight; we are not promoters. The entire onus of selling, collecting money, holding the money in hand, and turning it in—all of this clutters the mindset of the fighter. It puts a big portion of the pressure to sell the event on the fighter rather than on the promoter. If your individual ticket sales are down for whatever reason, you go into the fight knowing that your income is negatively affected. Promoters are even starting to require a minimum amount of ticket sales, and if you don't meet that goal, the value of unsold tickets comes out of your purse. This is an entire topic in itself, but that's a basic outline. For my fights in Altoona, we were able to sell 200 to 500 tickets, which is pretty darn good, and we had to collect all that money prior to each fight. What that means is that you are walking around with A LOT of cash, a large portion of it belonging to someone else. Having grown up in a middle-class household, I was never responsible for that much money in my life. I think the most ticket money we ever had at one time was $16,000 in green cash. It smelled so good! My family and I put together a nice team to see that everything was accounted for and delivered to the right place at the right time. My brother Ben, my dad, and my sister Nicki, in particular, really took care of things leading up to my fights back home.

What that means is that you are walking around with A LOT of cash.

I had fought at home in PA several times. I was starting to recognize the big picture of getting to the UFC, and it is more than just being a great fighter that gets you there. It's a combination of several factors working together. As in all facets of life, knowing the right people is very important. By this point in my career, Ben had taken over as the managerial figure. We never formally agreed to anything; I just remember his taking the phone one day and talking with a promoter. From then on, he was the man. Because I was fighting in my home state and having success, there was no real reason to sign with bigger management. My brother was able to get me the right fights at the right time for the right price. Allow me to explain something very important in professional combat sports: Many guys carry the bravado of "fighting anyone, anywhere, anytime." While this sounds "tough" and might make you look good in front of your friends, there is much more to it. Unlike wrestling, which was my upbringing, fighting requires a bit of molding for young fighters. Should a young fighter jump into high-level competition too early, a few losses could upset the entire path of his career. A good rule of thumb is that you incrementally test the young fighter, making each challenge a bit more difficult than the previous. At the same time, however, MMA is different from boxing in this regard. Boxers often reach records of 20-0 without fighting a single quality opponent. MMA lies somewhere in the middle.

I started my career without much thought. I didn't even really think of it as a "career." My first fight was against a black belt in Brazilian Jiu Jitsu (a form of ground fighting that stresses joint locks and choke holds), and my second fight was part of a big regional tournament (which I, thankfully, ended up winning). However, as my hobby began to bloom into a career, my team and I began putting more thought into whom and when I fought. We were able to take the right fights at the right times. As you approach the point of being signed by the UFC, or any other high-level organization, you really have to buckle down and make sure that the risks are worth the rewards when taking a fight. If you are one or two fights away from "getting signed" (shorthand for signing with the UFC), taking a very difficult regional fight can be risky. Sometimes, though, it's just what you need to get to that next level.

Timing is everything. I've heard countless accusations that I'm afraid of various fighters, but the truth is that I am guided by a smart, capable team who makes well thought-out decisions. And, for those who still think I'm afraid to fight anyone, look up two guys by the names of Johny Hendricks and Anthony Johnson, two of my past opponents.

ChAd

ChAd. What...or WHO, rather...is ChAd? Technically, ChAd is my Chief Advisor, my brother Ben, but really, ChAd is someone who has guided my career as if it were his own. The nickname has become a little joke in our family, but the meaning of the name couldn't be more spot-on. The idea of having a manager in MMA is confusing at times. To be a manager or an agent in most professional sports, you have to be qualified and credible. In fact, most managers have a law degree that helps when sifting through complicated contracts. Simply put, that is not always the case in MMA. While there are many quality managers in the sport (I was fortunate to have one of them), there are just as many who have no business calling themselves such. It's generally a friend helping out a friend, and, all of the sudden, he is a "manager." Or, it is a shyster who takes advantage of unassuming young fighters. The sport is new, and, in time, I'm sure this will work itself out for the better.

I went through the first part of my career without a manager. There was really no need. I wasn't making more than a few thousand dollars, and there wasn't much negotiation or opportunity for sponsorship. This went on for a few years, and as my career began to blossom and my stock increased, I quickly realized that I was anything but a good salesman and negotiator. One of my proudest moments as a salesman was selling a $20 shirt for $15 AFTER the transaction had been complete. I actually gave the person back five dollars for no reason at all. I just got nervous and said, "Here, take $5 back. I'll give it to you for $15." That pretty much sums up my salesmanship. Ben was taking notes, and before long, he intervened. He has no problem saying what needs to be said and doing what needs to be done. I'll someday take the reins and provide guidance and leadership for other young athletes, but for now, I am content being the athlete. Ben—ChAd rather—became my unofficial manager and dealt with the promoters leading up to my fights. He negotiated pay, opponents, and any other details that went along with securing a fight. I was in good hands—great hands— but it took me a few years and lot of experiences to realize just how fortunate I was.

Many people feel that mixing business and family

One of my proudest moments as a salesman was selling a $20 shirt for $15.

can lead to trouble, and while it's difficult to give an absolute response to that, I can say that in our situation it has worked successfully for years. I don't fully trust many people—really, really trust them. I have friends, and obviously family, in whom I confide, but, when it comes to business and money, I am extra careful. Okay, paranoid. A simple way I explain my relationship with ChAd is that I could give him the passwords to everything I hold secret and not think twice about it. I could give him full access to all of my accounts and not feel one ounce of worry. Many times, I don't even know how much money I am getting paid for sponsorships, and Ben will keep me updated along the way and ensure that the checks come in after the fight. It's nice to have an asset like him in doing business; he is ALWAYS looking out for my best interest. I've read many times that when you enter into a situation or business deal, you always have to consider the other person's perspective—what's in it for them. I have not the slightest doubt that the only thing in it for ChAd is my success.

I was more than happy to have Ben by my side. It was beneficial in so many ways. I had a trustworthy ally at all times, and it helped to bring us closer as brothers and friends. We cruised along like that for a few years. Later in my career, as I was approaching the UFC, we had to sit down and discuss taking on a manager. The obvious reality was that personal connections and relationships often determine why one fighter reaches the UFC and another, just as talented, might never reach that level. After some discussion, Ben and I thought it was in my best interest to assume a manager, and we made the decision that that manager would be Mike Constantino. MMA works like any business—connections are extremely important. Mike not only has those connections, but he also has a very thorough understanding of the business. Before I formally made any decisions, I spoke with Mike and Ben, letting Mike know that I wanted Ben involved in all of the decision-making, and letting Ben know that he was still going to be a vital part of my career. The two have harmoniously managed my career to this day. It's kind of funny (and at times annoying), but I am often the third person to know of any pertinent news in my career. Mike will find out the new information and call Ben. Because Ben knows how my mind works, he will offer up the best way to inform me. They will then conference-call with me to disclose the information in the predetermined manner. I used to get mad at this—being the third person to know about MY career—but in time, I've begun to appreciate it. I know that they are only looking out for me.

I am often the third person to know of any pertinent news in my career.

The biggest regret in my career is that I cannot give back to Ben all that he gives to me. I make a comfortable living fighting but not nearly as much as everyone thinks. I pay him for his work (um, kind of), but usually he refuses to take the money from me. I am adamant about it, though, so he accepts. It's my small way of saying thanks for everything that he does. If you would add up all the work and time he has put into my career, I'm sure that his net pay is deep into the negative, but that's not why he's in it. He is involved in my career out of a deep love and respect he has for what I am doing. He is like a parent in that respect. I've often told my wife that I think Ben hurts worse than I do when I lose and that I think he is happier than I am when I win. He could easily have been offended when Mike assumed my management, or resentful of the exposure that I've received, but he's not. He chooses to be the silent soldier always in my corner, ready to help me in any way that he can. As with Darcy and Dave, he realizes that sometimes you need to bring in people from the outside to keep pace with the progression of life and career.

I think Ben hurts worse than I do when I lose, and I think he is happier than I am when I win.

After my fights, I look at everything from the outside in; my feelings become once-removed. I see the joy in Ben, and in all of my family and friends for that matter, and I look at it as a job well done. That I am able to bring that much happiness and togetherness to those closest to me feels better than the actual intrinsic joy I feel from winning.

It's almost as if my purpose is not to be the best fighter I can be for my own benefit. Rather, it's to bring joy, satisfaction and sense of purpose to everyone around me. I get emotional when I sit back and look at everyone after my fights. They have been by my side through the entire journey, and it really doesn't matter to them whether I win or lose.

They'll always, always have my back.

Maybe there's no such thing as two keystones,
but here are mine: Ben and Mike.

CHANGES

My time on the road eventually started to take its toll on me, so I was about to make another move. While at ESU, I was introduced to AMA (American Martial Arts) Fight Club, which was much closer than Philly, "only" a one-hour commute each way from East Stroudsburg. So instead of making the two-hour+ trips to Philly and South Jersey, I started making the trip due west to Whippany, New Jersey. My career began to take shape at AMA. I was able to train more consistently, and I was always under the watchful eye of Mike, who was steadily helping me on my path to the UFC. I was making the trip to AMA 4 or 5 days a week while attending graduate school. Classes were at night, and training was during the day. It was a packed schedule.

At this time, I was exposed to a myriad of fighters—UFC guys, experienced veterans, wannabe fighters, you name it. We had a nice core of athletes at AMA. In addition, I leveraged my relationships with guys I had met to cross-train. South Jersey, NYC, CA, IL—I was taking full advantage of what the MMA world had to offer. With trips to Dan Handerson's Team Quest, Matt Hughes' HIT Squad, Renzo Gracie's, Ricardo Almeida's, I was literally training with THE BEST fighters in the world. These guys are Hall of Fame fighters; they laid the groundwork for the sport. It was as if this small-town PA boy had been picked up and transplanted into another world. I was eating lunch with legendary UFC Champion Matt Hughes, attending barbecues at Olympic-wrestler-turned-fighter Dan Henderson's ranch and listening to stories told by the one and only Renzo Gracie. I would make biweekly hour-and-a-half trips to Ricardo's gym in Hamilton, New Jersey. to double up on sparring and private boxing sessions, in addition to training at AMA. And we're not just talking sparring, we're talking SPARRING. I was going toe-to-toe with guys I had read about and watched on TV.

I was going toe-to-toe with guys I had read about and watched on TV.

As a guy who previously HATED fighting, I'm still amazed at the transition I made. And why did I make it? I don't know the exact answer, but there are two things that pop out. First, I saw my peers doing it and knew that I could follow in their footsteps. This was based on their skills in wrestling as compared to mine, and the work ethic I knew we shared, as nearly all high-level wrestlers do. Second, I never wanted to be afraid or uneasy about anything. I am an advocate of facing your fears head-on, and what better way to eliminate my fear of fighting than to fight the best fighters in the world on a daily basis? It just made sense.

I was honing my skills and finding my way several hours from home in New Jersey. And while there is nothing I enjoy more than being at home with family, when I set out on this journey, I was aware of the fact that it would most likely take me out of my comfort zone. I was ALWAYS in search of the best training throughout my entire career. Surround yourself with the best. I became a regular on the train that took me from New Jersey to New York City to get the best training I could. Here I was, Central PA through and through, who had maybe been to New York City once, becoming a regular on New Jersey/New York public transportation. On more than one occasion, I would chuckle to myself on my way over to Manhattan—I was so out of place, but I put on my "face." Everyone looks so mad and unhappy on the subways in New York, so as the old saying goes, "when in Rome ..." I looked as mad and unhappy as everyone else. I was used to looking people in the eyes back home, saying hello as I walked past. I still looked and nodded hello, but it was always a one-way conversation. Oh, well.

I'll never forget one of the coolest experiences in my life that happened at Renzo Gracie's gym in NY. Georges St. Pierre (GSP), probably the best fighter of all time, and Frankie Edgar were training for UFC title fights. It was not long after I had beaten Rick Story (that has its own chapter so stay tuned!), so I was at the highest point in my career. Every Monday, I would take the train into New York City for an afternoon class taught by John Danaher, a Brazilian Jiu Jitsu (BJJ) wizard who instructed the classes at Renzo's.

On this particular day, Danaher centered the entire training session around GSP, Frankie and... me. Here I was, one of three guys in the middle of the mats, surrounded by world-champion black belts, shoulder-to-shoulder with two of the biggest stars in MMA. I took a second to assess the situation, but only a second, because I was a piece of meat surrounded by a ravenous pride of lions. What followed was one of the most intense training sessions I can remember, and something I could've only dreamed about early on in my career.

I was a piece of meat surrounded by a ravenous pride of lions.

Although I traveled a good bit while being in New Jersey, my home base was AMA Fight Club. My trainager (trainer/manager), Mike, had a good read on where my career was heading, and he and my brother were working hard to get me to that next level. Our team at AMA didn't have the biggest stars when compared to other gyms around the country, but the way we trained and the people I trained with were second to none. There were ups and downs along the way, as with anything, but I was never alone at AMA. Our "pro training" met three or four times a week. I really believe AMA was a great fit for me. I am a hardheaded person, and I work as hard as anyone in the game, but I am also a sensitive person who appreciates the personal aspect of coaches, managers, teammates and others. If I had a problem, although it took some self-coaxing (I generally don't like conflict and can negotiate about as well as a penguin can fly), I would approach Mike, and as intimidating as he could be at times, he would always listen to what I said, and we've never had a problem that we couldn't solve. One of my biggest "non-negotiables" when I signed with Mike as a manager was that he include Ben in all of the decisions we made.

I was ultra-aware of not ditching the people who got me to where I was. Mike and Ben and I have worked as an awesome team over the years. Their habit of making me the third wheel in my fighting career caused me to developed a sense of anticipation when I would see that Mike or Ben was calling me, though, knowing that it was usually a piece of valuable information concerning my career and future. People came and went at AMA, but the core group of guys always stayed. Mike did an amazing job of bringing such great talent together to form a team. MMA is different from a normal sport. We are used to high school and college sports, where people show up every day during the season, and then there is an offseason. MMA is not like that. There are no seasons. When a guy fights, he could take off a week, or he could take off two months. Every guy has his own life situation— family, another job, whatever. But at AMA there were always guys in the room. Sometimes there may only be three or four of us, but everyone was there to help, and we'd get the job done.

It got lonely over in New Jersey, but I had several important people in my life who helped ease my transition. During this time period, I lived out of a suitcase. Generally, I would leave Amanda's home base of Middletown, PA, just outside of Harrisburg, at 6:30 AM Sunday morning for a week of training. After a 2.5 hour drive I would train at 10 AM in Whippany, New Jersey. After training, I would drive back to East Stroudsburg. I would spend the week training and driving all of PA/ NY/ NJ and then top it off with a Friday afternoon trip back to Middletown. This continued for a few years, but something needed to give. I couldn't keep this pace on the road. After a few years of talking about it, I finally made the move to East Hanover, New Jersey, a few miles away from AMA.

MY HISTORY IN EH

I had started making summer trips to East Hanover to do wrestling camps back around 2003. My college roommate, James LaValle grew up there, and through him, I met an entire community of people. The LaValles welcomed me into their home as if I were one of their own. I would spend entire Sundays at their home eating plate after plate of unbelievably delicious Italian food. If I needed something, either they would help me with it or direct me to someone who could. And, because I knew the LaValles, it got done. If you're not familiar with East Hanover, it's in Northern New Jersey and is extremely similar to the setting of the Sopranos. It was an awesome cultural experience. One of the people I met through the LaValles was Jackie. After years of commuting back and forth to East Hanover from East Stroudsburg, Jackie offered me a room at her place. Yes, she is a woman, and no, it wasn't awkward living with her. If Jackie wasn't such an awesome person, Amanda (still my girlfriend then) might have been a bit weary of my living with a woman. When I say that Jackie is one of the most selfless people I have ever met, that she is an incredible person and friend, it is all an understatement. She welcomed me into her home, put up with my manly things (stinky training gear, stinkiness in general, clutter), and most importantly, she genuinely welcomed me into her life. I became close friends with her friends, her family, and most of all, her. It was and is a great friendship. If it weren't for her, I would have never been able to live the life that I was living. The driving was adding up—financially, physically, and psychologically. She gave me a place to live seven minutes from AMA and 35 miles from New York City. I was in a much better training environment than I ever had been before.

I was adopted into one big extended family in New Jersey. Here I am with Jackie and Jionni.

THE UFC

On February 9, 2010, I signed with the Ultimate Fighting Championship (UFC). It also happened to be my 29th birthday. It was the culmination of a lifetime of hard work, dating back to when I started wrestling at eight years old. The 21 years of wrestling had molded me into the person I was and the fighter I was becoming. Signing with the UFC is the equivalent of playing in the Major Leagues or NFL. I was now at the top of my sport. I had just gotten there, but now it was about staying.

This is a good time to make a few distinctions. I touched on this at the beginning, but mixed martial arts (MMA) is the name of a sport, just like basketball or football. The UFC is the name of an organization or league, just like the NFL or MLB. For example, a person doesn't "fight UFC" just like they don't "play

NFL." MMA is the sport, and the UFC is the organization. (Hey, I'm all about teaching language.)

The UFC is viewed in different ways by different people. While it is the most prominent fighting promotion in the world, it has its naysayers. Many people claim the UFC is a giant monopoly that binds its fighters to unfair contracts based on its power and popularity in the fighting world. Personally, I can look at my time in the UFC without serious complaints. Yes, I was baptized by fire dealing with the brutal honesty that comes along with bad performances in the UFC, and I probably shed a tear or two because I felt my bosses could have had better bedside manner. But as I progressed through my career, I realized that I was a product within a business, and as with any other product, if I underperformed, I would suffer the consequences. In eleven fights with the UFC, I had some high highs and some low lows. I often refer to my fighting career as a big wave. I'd ride it until it reached the shore, and then I'd go out to find another.

It was the culmination of a lifetime of hard work, dating back to when I started wrestling at eight years old.

It all began on March 31, 2010, when I fought Jason High at Ultimate Fight Night 21 in Charlotte, NC. I was well-prepared, physically and mentally. I had reached the climax of my sport, and I was ready to make the most of my opportunity. The UFC has a system in place that ensures "fight week" runs smoothly. Fighters generally arrive on site five days prior to the event, and we use the next few days to do media, promos, open workouts and so on. I can remember that afternoon like it was yesterday. I had fought twelve times prior to my UFC debut, so the routine of fight day was familiar to me. The nerves I felt on that afternoon, however, were like nothing I had felt before. They were new and different. The scope of the situation was dawning upon us. Amanda and I took a walk in downtown Charlotte, and together we sat in awe and wonder at what was about to happen. The stage was much, much bigger than anywhere I had ever fought before.

In competition, there are two things that can happen when you feel nerves like this. They can scare you, negatively affecting your performance. Or you can feel those nerves, digest them, and harness them into positive energy that works in your favor. I was able to do the latter and come home with my first UFC win. Jason High was a decorated wrestler as well. He came into this fight just as I did, a newbie in the UFC. After 15 minutes of back and forth action, I was able to scramble and control my way to a unanimous decision victory. I controlled the vast majority of the fight, but I will note here that in the last 20 seconds of the fight, I nearly blew it. Jason is well known for his guillotine choke, a maneuver in which you snap your opponent's head down and wrap your arms around his neck, creating a guillotine-like predicament. I was dangerously close to celebrating my victory just a tad too early, a valuable lesson I would not soon forget. I squirmed my way out of danger, however, and walked out of the Octagon as the victor.

One of my coolest experiences in the UFC was
fighting in front of the troops at Fort Hood, TX.
Especially with family and friends there to support me.
Beside me above is my brother Scott in his
Army Combat Uniform.

For the next three years, I was a UFC fighter. I
learned so much about the industry and life in general
during my first UFC tenure. I alternated wins and
losses in my next four fights, and I stayed true to what
got me there, wrestling. I was able to take down nearly
everyone I fought, even NCAA champion and future
UFC champion Johny Hendricks. My wrestling-heavy
style was bringing criticism from some fans and
industry people alike. People tend to favor two guys
standing in front of each other slugging it out. For
better or worse, I am not one of those guys. My goal is

to win fights and avoid taking abuse. Granted, this is a combat sport, and you are going to get hit, sometimes very hard, but I had to aim for a better calculation than a 50/50 chance of delivering or suffering a knockout. My wrestling style was helping me advance my career. I train every aspect of the sport, and I invest 100% of my energy into evolving as a fighter, but I will always stick to my roots. If a fighter has wrestled for 20 years and boxed for 3 years, why not go with your strength? It worked for me. I fought on the undercards of big Pay-Per-View events, and I even co-headlined a few UFC events on live television. I was on my way to the biggest night of my fighting career and one of the biggest nights of my life. But, first, I'd have one of the biggest tests of any kind that I ever faced.

WHAT'S AN INFARCT?

On February 28, 2011, I woke up in my apartment in New Jersey. Just like any other Monday, I was headed into NYC to train. On this particular morning, however, my life would be changed forever. I awoke around 8:00 a.m. and proceeded to the bathroom for my morning routine. What happened next was something I had never experienced before and will hopefully never experience again. After flushing the toilet, I turned to wash my hands at the sink. During the transition, I was hit with the most powerful wave of dizziness and nausea that I had ever felt. The room immediately began to spin at a rapid pace, and I had broken into the most intense sweat of my life. Within ten seconds, my light gray sweatpants were dark gray, completely drenched with sweat. My entire body was soaking wet. I couldn't stand up, so I hunched over on the floor next to the toilet. The room hadn't slowed down, and my equilibrium was completely off. I jostled around as best I could and sprawled out on the bathroom floor, my eyes shut. I was completely at the mercy of whatever had taken over my body. Thankfully, Jackie was home from work that day. I managed to murmur her name. She came running to the bathroom to find me lying on my back, writhing. We were both in a state of shock and confusion. I wouldn't say panic because we were both relatively calm, but we were completely astounded by the situation. She asked if I wanted her to call an ambulance, and I remember the weirdest thought popping into my head. I thought back to when I fractured my orbital socket, that I had learned that insurance doesn't always cover the cost of the ambulance ride to the hospital. Here I was, possibly on the brink of death for all we knew, and I was worried about paying a few hundred dollars for an ambulance ride. My eyes remained shut to combat the nausea from the spinning room. The scariest part, perhaps, was when I felt an awkward sensation in my tongue. I said to Jackie, "I think my tongue is going numb." It was at this point the seriousness of the situation set in. I recalled that numbness in the tongue is often associated with a stroke. We were both scared. Jackie

The scariest part, perhaps, was when I felt an awkward sensation in my tongue. I said to Jackie, "I think my tongue is going numb."

repeated the idea of calling an ambulance.

To this day, I cannot definitively say why I didn't choose to go to the hospital. I'm not sure if it is my innate will to never accept defeat, or if it was just a random decision in the heat of the moment. But for whatever reason, I opted to stay at Jackie's and wait it out. We still had no idea what was going on. Assisted by Jackie, I crawled across the hallway and into the guest room, or "Stroke Room" as it came to be known. For the next three days, I laid in bed, sweating, eyes shut, and unable to eat or drink. I cannot explain the intensity of dizziness and nausea that I felt. Every time I would tilt my head left or right, I would vomit. I had to lie flat on my back, eyes pointed at the ceiling, still shut. Jackie was endlessly helpful that week. From supplying vomit buckets, to escorting me to the bathroom, to changing my sheets, to buying me Gatorade and Pedialite Pops. Her grandma even came over with some fresh soup to help. Jackie resumed work on Tuesday.

For three solid days, the room never stopped spinning, and my nausea didn't let up even a bit. I didn't want to worry my family, four-and-half hours away in PA, so I waited until I could at least speak with a bit of clarity before I called. Amanda recalls speaking with me that week, unable to hear or comprehend what I was saying. My mother urged me to come home, but I felt better about staying in New Jersey. After three days of lying in bed vomiting and sweating, I finally felt a bit of relief. Exhausted, stiff and sore, I needed a shower. I mustered up enough energy to get to the bathroom, but I could barely manage to disrobe and get into the tub. All I could do was sit down and let the water run over my body.

On Thursday evening, Jackie took me to an emergency care facility in the area. I was feeling noticeably better, but it was apparent something was still wrong. I was able to stand up and slowly walk with assistance, but I still wasn't feeling normal. The doctor diagnosed me with vertigo, but I knew it was more than that. I learned several extremely valuable life lessons through this ordeal, one of them being that regardless of what certain people tell you, experts or otherwise, sometimes YOU know best what's going on with YOUR body. I am not an expert by any means, but sometimes you just know, and I knew. On Friday of that week, I drove home to PA. Amanda and I had planned to look at potential wedding locations. I shouldn't have driven. I was barely able to turn my head left and right to look for cars while changing lanes. I sat at our wedding meeting in a daze. After a few more days, I resumed training, but I still wasn't feeling right. I decided to get an MRI.

A call from the doctor at 10:30 AM on a Sunday is never good.

A week later, I was sparring on a Sunday morning when the doctor called. A call from the doctor at 10:30 AM on a Sunday is never good. My MRI results had come back abnormal. It showed an infarct in the right cerebellar region of my brain. A what? An infarct, I learned, is scar tissue on the brain. Although mine was very small, it signified that blood flow had been cut off to a certain part of my brain for a period of time. Fortunately, since the area was so small, my brain was able to recover and build new pathways for the blood to travel. What I also learned was that infarct is basically another way to say stroke. Stroke is a very powerful word, especially when you're a young person; it hit me like a ton of bricks. I was a 29-year-old professional athlete and in the best shape of my life. I have never done a single drug in my life, and I only sparingly drink alcohol.

For the next six weeks, I underwent test after test: MRI, MRA, EKG, Echo, you name it. I even went to Pittsburgh to see a hematologist for blood testing. I brought my results to two different neurologists, and all of the doctors said the same thing: "We can see nothing that would indicate why you had the stroke." It was a mystery.

When you're a lifelong athlete, and then all of a sudden, you're not, it's tough to deal with.

Not only was I worried about my health and overall wellness, but I had no idea what this meant in terms of my career. Fighting was my livelihood, how I made my living. It was also my identity. When you're a lifelong athlete, and then all of a sudden, you're not, it's tough to deal with, but you must develop a new identity and purpose. This had happened to me once before with wrestling, but I was fortunate to find MMA. I wasn't yet prepared to find the next "next thing." I stayed up night after night, worrying and traveling back and forth between New

Jersey and PA for all kinds of doctor appointments. Finally, after all of the testing and waiting, there was light at the end of the tunnel. With the very clear determination that my stroke had nothing to do with combat sports, and I was at no higher risk than the average fighter, I was given clearance by both neurologists to continue training and fighting. I had no restrictions whatsoever. I held those letters of clearance as if they were gold.

After evaluating all of my test results, there were no conclusive links that showed the cause of the stroke, but they were able to conclude it was not due to trauma. I was very hesitant and nervous to resume my training, but at the same time, I was very confident in my doctors' advice and expertise. As a professional fighter, I can't help but consider how I treat my body and my brain; it would be irresponsible not to. After I am done fighting, I will still be a person, a father, a husband, and everything else I plan to be, so it's extremely important that I balance my passion with objective decision-making. This experience was a big reality check, but with the help of those closest to me, I decided to move forward with my career.

THE STORY STORY

June 26, 2011. Pittsburgh, PA. Sometimes in life, things just happen. We have no control over the fate that awaits us. Some of us (including me) are inclined to call it destiny. We are just passengers on our own predetermined journey. My fate on June 26, 2011, would change my life. I arrived in Pittsburgh on the Wednesday of fight week. I was scheduled to fight TJ Grant, another UFC welterweight who unbeknownst to us had fallen ill just a few days prior. Mike and I arrived at the airport and headed to the fighter hotel. Upon arrival, we immediately checked in with the UFC, I hopped on the scale to check my weight. It is standard practice for me to be anywhere from ten to fifteen pounds over the contracted weight five days prior to the fight. Some fighters are more than twenty pounds over their weight class. I can only speak for myself, but I have a system in place to ensure I make weight while putting the least amount of stress on my body. It comes with twenty years of experience and trial and error. I could write another book (and maybe I will) on the technical side of making weight and feeling prime for competition, but for now, let's get back to Pittsburgh. After hopping on the scale, I signed 100 or so posters to be given away, and then Mike and I were on our own. We collected our room keys and got situated. We were killing time wandering around the hotel when his phone rang. It was Joe Silva, the UFC matchmaker.

Joe is the guy who hires and fires you. He is one of the top dogs. When he calls, your ears perk up. My first impulse was negative, but Mike showed no concern. He answered his phone and said, despairingly, "No way, are you serious?" He looked to me and said, "No fight. TJ got sick and never got on the plane." My heart sank. The fight was so close to home. I had hundreds of people coming to watch me fight on the biggest stage of my life. I was devastated. The kicker was that I had to stick around for the week and make weight in order to get my "show" money (fighters generally get paid to show up and fight, and then if you win, you get paid a "win" bonus). This meant that I had to go through the miserable weight cut for no real reason. Yes, I would be paid, but it's not just about being paid. It's about showing off all the hard work you put into training.

I had two choices. I could accept that I wasn't fighting and cut weight in an unhealthy manner. Or I could stay the course, maintain my regular fight week schedule, and keep hoping that somehow I'd be fighting. This goes back to how I was raised. My parents instilled in me the importance of doing what's right, taking the road less traveled. It would've been easier to binge and purge to make weight, but that would hurt my performance should I compete. I decided to stay the course, stick to my normal fight week routine, and if it proved to be fruitless, I could look at myself in the mirror and know that I was as prepared as possible. In hindsight, it was at this point, I believe, that fate was beginning to show its face.

We woke the next day with no real expectation of getting a fight, just a small gleam of hope. Then Joe Silva called. He had found me a matchup against another strong wrestler looking to break into the UFC. But there was a catch; the fight was to be contested at 175 pounds, five pounds above my weight class. In addition, my proposed opponent was coming down from middleweight, the weight class above welterweight. It is in these situations where it is important to have a good team around you. My immediate instinct was to take the fight. I had hundreds of people coming to watch me, and I'd most likely never fight again in the UFC so close to home. It was an opportunity I did not want to miss. But after examining every possible angle with Mike and Ben, we decided against taking the fight. As a fighter, it's tough to look at the situation from the outside in. We just want to fight. To have smart, genuine people around

It was at this point, I believe, that fate was beginning to show its face.

you is invaluable. Sometimes they protect us from ourselves. It was an extremely difficult decision to make, but we made it as a team, and we stuck by it. We kept hoping, but nothing materialized. So there I was, still with no fight, empty and hopeless. It's a complex thing, fighting. You have to do what's best for yourself, but at the same time, because it's a public sport and business, every decision you make is dissected in the public eye.

Later that day, we were cutting weight in the sauna when Mike took note of a small, subtle interaction just a few feet away. He kept it to himself. It was nothing major, just the manner in which two people were talking outside of the sauna. It was Rick Story and his trainer. Rick was scheduled to fight Nate Marquardt in the main event in the welterweight division. He was on a six–fight win streak. If he beat Marquardt, he would be next in line to fight Georges St. Pierre for the world title. Rick Story is an animal. Quiet, muscled, he's the type of person you don't want to mess with in or out of a dark alley. Little by little, we began to hear rumors that Nate Marquardt might not pass his prefight physical, and the main event would be off. In our eyes, the odds of Marquardt's not passing the physical were slim to none, so I tried my best to keep myself in check. At one point during the week, we went to Primanti Brothers, a Pittsburgh sandwich gem. Meat, cheese, French fries, cole slaw—a weight-cutter's best friends! I was just sitting there staring, miserably craving a sandwich. I actually contemplated devouring a sandwich or two, then pulling the trigger to get it back out. I still had to make weight, and if I didn't have to perform, who cares how I got there? It was only a few more days of sacrifice, so I chose to hold off. By Thursday and Friday of that week, though a few rumors were still bouncing around, we had pretty much accepted that I had no fight. I posted a video on my website explaining the situation. You could see the pain and frustration in my face. I have always been very active on my website and social media channels to keep my fans informed. I waited as long as I could, but I had to let everyone know the fight was off. (You can actually follow a chronological timeline of my career by following my blog and social media links at www.charlie-brenneman.com).

This was my chance to shine in front of my hometown fans.

The week was coming to a close. Friday is typically when the real weight cut begins, and Saturday is the weigh-in. (This was a Sunday night fight, rather than Saturday night, so the days are pushed back one). Friday arrived, and there was no mention of Marquardt's potential commission troubles. The wave of excitement had subsided, and disappointment had set in. I was now just going through the motions to make weight. My fans were out of the loop as well; we weren't able to disclose any of this. They knew I wasn't fighting, but there was no mention of Marquardt. The web would have exploded with all kinds of "journalism" about the situation. Most of my fans had decided not to make the trip to Pittsburgh. Hollidaysburg, my hometown, is about two hours east of Pittsburgh. Being a Central PA guy, this was my chance to shine in front of my hometown fans, to be the local favorite. Friday night came and went.

Saturday was weigh-in day. After the morning weight cut, we typically rest for a few hours before heading to the weigh-in location. We hadn't heard anything new or valuable on the situation for a day or so. It was as if I had been forgotten. The UFC had a thousand things to do, and I was the least of their concerns. My weight came off easily, as it normally did, and I was ready to receive my "show" money. The weigh-in normally takes place at 4 PM. Prior to departing the hotel for the weigh-in, all fighters and cornermen check in to ensure that everyone is present. To show you how much of an afterthought I was to this event, get this: When Burt, the on-site boss of fight week, finished reading off the checklist, I was left standing on the sidewalk. I wasn't the last one picked; I wasn't picked at all. "Ahem," I said, "Burt, which bus do I go on?" "Ahh, just pick one," he said. Fast-forward a half hour, and we are at Heinz Field for weigh-ins. Before you are actually cleared to fight, each fighter must undergo a brief physical examination prior to weighing in. As everyone's name was getting called to go see the doctor, I was twiddling my thumbs in the back, not sure of what to do or where to go. This is no fault of the UFC. I was now just a non-factor in the event. Mike, Ben and I were just hanging out trying to make the best of the situation.

Mike is a very observant person. He often refers to his past as an Executive Protection Specialist, a fancy way of saying bodyguard. If it looks like he's not paying attention to you, it's because he's scanning the situation, dissecting people and locating all possible points of exit. President Obama happened to be staying at our hotel that week, and before anyone knew, Mike had taken note of an increase in security on the premises; he's good. While we were standing backstage of weigh-ins, forgotten, he noticed a small conversation taking place amongst the UFC brass. Also involved in that conversation was Greg Sirb, the head of the PA State Athletic Commission. (Athletic commissions oversee everything in regard to a sanctioned MMA event. They can deem any athlete eligible or ineligible, and their decision supersedes that of the UFC). He continued to observe, not mentioning any of this to Ben or me. Finally, Mike filled us in on the details. We began to build hope. When the men finished their conversation, they immediately located me, and I was told to go get my prefight physical. What a change in direction this day was taking. This was a step in the right direction, but nothing was set. As you can imagine, my adrenaline began to flow; I noted to the doctor that my heart rate would most likely be elevated.

As I was undergoing my physical in the makeshift office, Mike burst through the curtain and shouted, "It's on!!!" Oh. My. God. Here I was being thrust into the spotlight as the co-main event of a live UFC show on Versus TV. Our fight was now being billed as the co-main event, while another fight was bumped up to the main event slot. The UFC was taking a big risk in putting me on this big of a stage, so it made sense to move us to the co-main spot. When I finished my physical, I had to hurry to my spot in line. I hopped in front of Story, and the adventure officially began. (I don't have the exact details of why Marquardt was ineligible, so I don't want to speculate. An Internet search can point you in the right direction).

Nerves are interesting. I had a habit of letting them get the best of me in wrestling. I would worry myself into a state of uncertainty and self-doubt. While the physical aspect of sports is important, the mental aspect is even more important. You can be 100% physically prepared for a competition, but if your mind is elsewhere, you might as well pack up and head home. I have learned the hard way that your mind is much more powerful than your body. It goes back to my wrestling career. Wrestling is like no other sport in the world. The mental and physical toll that it takes on your mind and body is unmatched. Intense workouts are the least of it. Cutting weight teaches you mental fortitude that can't be attained otherwise. Sitting with an empty plate at Thanksgiving and Christmas, watching everyone eat and enjoy himself in the school cafeteria, sucking on ice cubes at parties—so many memories. But I'd never change them, not for anything in the world. They made me who I am.

I am a much stronger person because of wrestling, and I could never give back what it has given to me. It was through wrestling and maturity that I was able to

You can be 100% physically prepared for a competition, but if your mind is elsewhere, you might as well pack up and head home.

build a strong mental capacity in regard to competition, and that would be a huge asset here in Pittsburgh. You always hear "Stay calm in case of an emergency." That advice is based on fact. Your body changes when you begin to lose control. Blood flow, body temperature, and loss of clear thought are just a few effects that can negatively affect you. In sports your nerves can destroy you, and many times, your dreams. Everyone has nerves. Not everyone makes the most of them. Fortunately, on June 26, 2011, my nerves went into battle for me, not against me.

Everyone has nerves. Not everyone makes the most of them.

At this point, I began to feel a sense of peace and clarity. It was as close to an out-of-body experience as I've ever had. I was becoming a piece of the already foregone conclusion that was developing before my eyes. I was going to win this fight. So many factors had fallen into place. The stars were aligned in my favor. There was no other explanation. From TJ's getting sick, to my not taking the replacement fight, to Marquardt's medical problem, to Story's agreeing to take the fight, things were just falling into place. Perhaps the most vital piece to this puzzle was Dana White's decision to ultimately allow this matchup to take place. He was basing an entire event around a guy who had yet to prove himself on the big stage. The UFC had spent months building an entire event around the Story/Marquardt matchup, and now they were thrusting a relative "no name" into the spotlight. Greg

Sirb, who is as tough as any commissioner out there, even helped assure Dana that I was a worthy opponent. I had fought several times in front of Greg Sirb in my previous fights in PA. He is a tough, no-nonsense man who will tell it like it is. I had proven my worth to him, thankfully. You never know when something you do, or say, at one point in time can have a profound effect you in the future. Take note, kids. Brenneman vs. Story was set.

We had an awesome post-weigh-in dinner at The Cabana Bar in Pittsburgh. It was extra-special because several members of the Iraq and Afghanistan Veterans of America (IAVA), a sponsor of mine, came to hang out and enjoy the evening. Team Spaniard was there in full force—friends, family, and fans.

Following a week of stress, it was great to be surrounded by everyone. I vividly remember my legs throbbing that night at dinner; I was being pulled in many directions and didn't have a chance to really sit down and rest. My legs are also the first thing to go when nerves start to set in, but these were natural nerves, the ones that come along with fighting in front of upwards of a million people on live TV. They would not affect my performance. I went to bed that night flying high. Amanda and I shared a room with my brother and his wife, Meghan. (Ben comes to all of my fights.)

I woke the next morning at 7:30 AM. On fight day, I try to sleep in as long as possible, but not on this fight day. As soon as I opened my eyes, the gravity of the situation hit me like a ton of bricks. I lay there, wide-eyed and staring at the ceiling, waiting for

Amanda to wake up. When she awoke, the first words out of my mouth were, "Oh my God, I can't believe this is happening." At that point, I strapped on my seatbelt and went for the ride of my life.

Midway through fight day, I relinquished my hold on the present. I knew that God and the universe would not have put me in this situation to lose. I am a religious person, and I also believe in forces of nature. June 26, 2011, was my day. Warming up for the fight, I felt fresh and relaxed. I was actually smiling in the locker room—a real smile, not something I was manufacturing to hide my true feelings. There were so many positives in this situation. We were in Pittsburgh; I had hundreds of personal fans there to see me. I was in a total win–win situation; and, on top of that, I was representing Sheetz. Sheetz is a mainstay in my neck of the woods, a humble dairy store turned best convenience store ever, and I

There is this feeling of invincibility, that there is no one IN THE WORLD who can stop you.

had grown up with members of the Sheetz family. I have a very fond opinion of their family and business, so representing them on a national stage was awesome.

A few minutes before walking out to my fight, however, I was told that I wasn't able to wear my Sheetz walkout shirt to the cage. We were literally in the locker room, moments before walking out to fight in front of thousands of people, and we were dealing with sponsor issues. Sponsorships are a big thing in

MMA. It's how we make a good portion of our income. But, to wear a brand into the Octagon, it needs to be approved by the UFC. In some instances, the sponsor even has to pay the UFC for the ability to sponsor a fighter. Well, we had gone through the appropriate channels of getting everything approved, but it didn't matter. This was just a bad situation. Mike and Ben did their best to keep the issue hidden from me as they sorted things out with the UFC. I did my best to stay focused and continue my warm up, and thankfully, the issue was resolved. Thank you, Mike. Thank you, Ben.

Walking out to the cage is a unique experience with each fight. Sometimes I am so over-the-top excited and pumped up that I don't know what I'm doing; I am just on autopilot. There is this feeling of invincibility, that there is no one IN THE WORLD who can stop you. And those are not just words to fill a page; you really and truly believe that no one on the face of this earth can stand in your way. And, other times, your physical body is walking down the aisle to a fight, surrounded by thousands of screaming fans, but your mind is as cool as can be, as if you were taking a stroll around the block. On the other side of 27 professional fights, I have learned to just "let it be." Whatever comes naturally to me at that moment is what I harness and follow. There are times when I'm in the perfect zone, and I inadvertently take note of a small detail that snaps me right out of it.

One of those times was on my way to the cage in Pittsburgh. I was totally focused on the here and now, amped and ready, when I happened to glance to my right and see my friend Matt Anderson just before I got to the cage. As soon as I saw him, I thought, "Oh, hey Matt, what's up?" "Get back in the zone!" I immediately shouted to myself. "We are in Pittsburgh to do a job!" (If I ever looked right through you at an event, now you know why. Nothing personal!)

So there I was, in the cage and ready to go. By far, this was the biggest stage I had ever been on in my life. Would it be fight or flight? I fought, and I fought well. It went just how we had planned. I was able to use my superior wrestling and pressure to grind Story down each round. While my striking is not my strongest part of the game, I am able to set up takedowns with strikes as well as anyone in the sport. Story had no answer for it. I was ahead by two rounds heading into the third. It was back and forth in that final round, and for the first time, I was put into a few precarious situations. But I kept moving and never accepted anything but victory. When the final bell rang, I felt as euphoric as I've ever felt in my entire life. The way I explain it is this ... imagine there is a thing in the world that you want more than anything else, the daily fantasy that you replay over and over every day—an experience, an object, a million dollars, whatever it may be. Then imagine someone just hands it to you.

All I could repeat to myself was, "Is this real? Is this really happening?"

You have that thing that you wanted more than anything in the world. It was like a fantasy playing out in real life, except no one gave it to me—I earned it.

For the post-fight interview, I spoke with Joe

Rogan. THE Joe Rogan (famous actor, comedian and UFC commentator). Every fighter dreams of being interviewed by Joe Rogan after a ginormous UFC victory. All I could repeat to myself was, "Is this real? Is this really happening?" I was an overnight rock star. Phone calls, interviews, guest appearances, you name it. I was now known in the world of mixed martial arts. And, perhaps even more importantly, Dana White knew my name. You'd think that was already a given, but it's not. While some fighters maintain a personal relationship with Dana and the Fertitta brothers (UFC owners), a vast majority of us do not. In MMA, even more so in the UFC, it is very much about what you've done lately. You can be hot today and gone tomorrow. The industry will continue with or without you. It really makes no difference, so you might as well make the most of it while you're there.

That night, the next day, and for an entire month, it didn't slow down. The media had never really cared whether I won or lost, plus or minus an article or two. Now I was on the front page of every major MMA media site. I saw the direct effect immediately. You're treated differently—much, much better. In professional sports, you are directly worth your performance. And for now, my performance was great. Man was it wonderful. I was now ranked seventh in the world.

UPS AND DOWNS

Following the Story fight, I alternated wins and losses for the next year. After my win in Pittsburgh, I fought Anthony "Rumble" Johnson later that year in October. "Rumble" is known for being the biggest welterweight in the sport, and he has a history of coming into fights overweight. It would be much easier if I could use that as an excuse in our fight, but he did indeed make the welterweight limit of 171 pounds. (As I am revising this book, he is scheduled to fight Jon Jones for the UFC Light Heavyweight Championship—that's at 205 lbs.!). It didn't help matters that I was one of the smaller welterweights in the UFC. The fact that weigh-ins take place 24 hours prior to the fight also worked against me. That was just another 24 hours for him to get back to his normal size. It's nothing for a fighter to gain 10-15 pounds between weigh-ins and the fight, mostly just water weight, and the rumor was that "Rumble" entered the cage at 200 lbs. or more on fight night. Though it sounds impossible, it's not. Many fighters take pride in how much weight they put on post weigh-ins, often posting pictures online. As a result of his size, this was the first fight in my career where I actually felt the punches, repeating "ouch" in my head every time he landed one. Normally, you just feel impact, not actual pain. Your adrenaline temporarily masks the pain, but once the adrenaline subsides, the pain emerges.

I ended up losing to "Rumble" by TKO and then won my next fight in Nashville, Tennessee. Nashville was my favorite trip of them all. The electricity in that town is awesome. I won my fight on a Friday, and we stayed in Nashville for the weekend. Honky tonk bars, BBQ, the Country Music Hall of Fame, we did it all.

I earned a nice payday that night, and my "financially efficient" self (some may say cheap) splurged and bought Amanda a $230 pair of good old authentic Nashville cowboy boots. It felt good to be able to do something like that for her. Though it was a simple pair of boots, it was a small way of saying, "Thank you for supporting me over the years." At that point, I hoped to, one day, give her a beautiful house, but for then, boots had to do. I returned to New Jersey and got back to training. My next fight would take place on June 8, 2012, but my life was about to take another turn, and this one doesn't have a happy ending.

A WALKING ANGEL

There are some people on this earth who are truly walking angels. I was fortunate to meet and become great friends with one such man. When I left Hollidaysburg to pursue fighting, my first stop was East Stroudsburg, PA. While getting my master's degree at ESU, I wasn't yet able to sustain myself on fighting alone. I continued to work in education, substitute-teaching to make ends meet. Every morning on the drive to school, I would pass a small personal training studio with the big words "No Limits Personal Training" proudly displayed on the building façade. I must've driven passed the sign a hundred times before I finally convinced myself to give them a call. After a few rings, the machine picked up and a voice exploded with enthusiasm. "Hi, this is Don Messing of No Limits Personal Training. Leave a message, and we'll get back to you. Make it a great day! The choice is yours!" I was taken aback by the genuine enthusiasm I heard in his voice.

My first impression of Don, just from listening to that recording, was spot on. After some back and forth, I stopped by No Limits to inquire about training at his gym. He was more than happy to start working with me in a one-on-one training environment. One-on-one training is very expensive, and at this time, I was making a comfortable income, but I didn't have extra to spare. There is a common misconception that most fighters make a lot of money. Yes, in the UFC, I've had some nice paydays, but, after management, training fees and, of course, taxes, I've been able to maintain a comfortable middle class living. Fighting at the highest level is expensive, and on top of that, if you lose a fight, you make half as much as if you had won. Money was not important to Don; in exchange for training me, we agreed that I would represent Don and No Limits Personal Training in everything I did—social media, fight gear, and so on. Don saw it as an investment. He appreciated my work ethic and the intrinsic value of working with such a committed athlete.

There are some people on this earth who are truly walking angels.

In a short time, though, it became much more than just helping a kid pursue his dream. Don became one of my best friends, and I one of his. We were constantly together, and I was becoming a bigger, stronger athlete. The training was new and valuable. We worked on agility drills that I'd never done before.

He was completely open-minded. With such a strenuous training schedule, it is essential that I am mentally challenged by my workouts. I can't do the same thing over and over again. Don was great at mixing in new, purposeful exercises to accommodate me, but at the same time, he was the boss, not I.

With Don at No Limits Personal Training.

Our friendship extended outside of the gym, too. It was my first time living away from home permanently, and it got lonely at times. Don invited me into his life. He was the most active person I've ever met. He would wake up at 4 AM, work out, and then start his first appointment by 5 or 5:30. IF he had any breaks in the day, he filled it with something—mountain biking, kayaking, off-roading in his souped-up Jeep; he would never sit and waste time. His afternoons and evenings were filled with clients, and his "days" wouldn't end until 7:30 p.m. most nights. From there, he'd hurry home to get a quick bite to eat and cap the day off with the love of his life, Carrie. It was amazing to see him use every single minute of his existence for good. He was an inspiration.

Don worked out daily, did all kinds of outdoor activities, and he was also very involved in competitive bodybuilding. His meals were neatly packed and prepared in Tupperware containers on a regular basis. He would indulge now and again, but for the most part, he was extremely strict with his diet. Don said something simple, yet profound to me one day. Sitting at the gym between clients, he was eating a plain rice cake, no flavor, just a plain white rice cake. He was making "ooh" and "ahh" sounds at how good it was. I was bewildered at how such a simple, bland snack could be so good. I asked him, "Is it really that good, or are you just telling yourself that it's that good?" In his response, he quipped, "Isn't that the same thing?" It was the first time I realized just how programmable our own minds can be.

Unlike many people whose goals are also to help others, Don lived and breathed that mission every day of his life. He gave and gave and gave.

Through our work together, Don was quickly becoming a fan of MMA. He had a history of kickboxing and martial arts, so it was exciting for him to get back in the mix. He began to work with other fighters in the area, too, and, before long, No Limits was the mainstay for MMA strength and conditioning in the East Stroudsburg area. Don was a visionary. His goal in life was to help others. And, unlike many people whose goals are also to help others, Don lived and breathed that mission every day of his life. He gave and gave and gave.

Sometimes, it even crosses my mind that he was too generous. He was so giving to other people that he often neglected his own feelings and needs. When I say he was an angel on earth, it's not hyperbole. He used his position in life to help every person he could possibly reach. And, through all of us, he has impacted thousands and thousands of lives for the better.

The biggest gift I was able to give Don, I would say, was having him in my corner at the Rick Story fight. You only get three spots in your corner. Ben was always one; Mike was always one; and that third spot changed depending on the fight. I've tried to rotate between important people in my life—my family, Darcy and so on. I couldn't have picked a better fight to have Don as my third cornerman.

As I said before, Don and I were great friends, and he was so giving and selfless in our friendship that I sometimes look back and feel guilty. He wasn't just a great friend/mentor/trainer, but he was also a father–figure away from home. Two instances stick out in my mind that really show Don's overall goodness. For my birthday one year, Don bought me a first-class Columbia jacket completely out of nowhere. It easily cost several hundred dollars. He saw an opportunity to blow me away with an awesome gift, and he pounced on it. He didn't need to spend that kind of money on a friend's birthday gift, but he knew how much I'd appreciate it. I laugh at it now, but he made me promise not to tell Carrie about the jacket. Secondly, I had been pining over a Russell Simmons brand chain for a few years. It was very fancy and a bit out of my normal style—a big, silver, very blingy cross, but it was something I wanted. At $275, I was waiting for the right time to make the purchase. Out of the blue one day, I walked into the gym, and there it was. That's the kind of person Don was. I couldn't come close to keeping up with his generosity, so I just did my best to become a better person due to his presence.

On June 8, 2012, I was scheduled to fight Erik Silva in Fort Lauderdale, Florida. Don and Carrie were to make the long trip from PA to see the fight. Our training camp was great. He was so excited about coming to Florida. Don hardly ever took a break from work, so having a UFC weekend in Ft. Lauderdale was perfect for him. It was a typical fight week. That week, weigh-ins were on Thursday and the fight on Friday. I went to bed Wednesday night feeling good, approximately five pounds overweight. I woke up around 7:30 that next morning, and as usual, I grabbed my phone for my morning Internet rundown/social media sweep. But, this time, there was a missed call from Carrie, Don's wife. It was very strange.

I just did my best to become a better person due to his presence.

She never called me, much less so early in the morning. Almost simultaneously, as I clicked to listen to Carrie's voicemail, Amanda, doing her own Internet rundown said in an eerily shaky voice, "Oh my God, Charlie." I then listened to Carrie's shaky voice telling me to call her immediately. I looked at Amanda with a pit in my stomach. She turned her phone and showed me a Facebook post. Don had passed away in the night. My heart sank. I was numb.

Forget about the fight, I had just lost a close friend. My mind was running in a thousand directions. Fight? Don't fight? Fly home? I left the room and sat in the hallway. I was not immediately emotional, just void of feeling. I couldn't believe it. Don was the most health-conscious person in my life. As I sat outside the room, Amanda informed my brother what had happened. He contacted Mike, and the two of them just let me be for a while. But there was an issue at hand that had to be addressed. First, I had to cut the remaining five pounds to make weight later that day; as if cutting weight weren't bad enough, I now had to do it with a heavy heart. And, second, was I still even going to fight? I wasn't in a position to just take my time and see how I felt. My decision would have a ripple effect, so I didn't have the luxury of letting my feelings process naturally. People were depending on me to fight Erick Silva that next day. It wasn't just Silva; it was the UFC and everyone else who was tuning in to watch the event. We were the co-main event bout, and a lot of preparation goes into setting that up. If we scrapped the fight, the UFC would need to find a quick replacement, shoot new promos, rearrange the card— all of these things hinged on my decision. I'm not trying to sound cliché or overdramatic, but if it were up to Don, in that moment, he would have wanted me to take that fight and perform to the best of my abilities, flying proudly the No Limits flag. I took the fight, but I didn't perform. I'll say more about that shortly.

The entire experience in Florida taught me a very valuable lesson dealing with the mind. Looking back, I am glad I took the fight. It was the right thing to do. However, in evaluating my performance, it was pretty easy to see the major error I made in mental execution. At this point in my career, my mental game had developed much more in fighting than it ever had in wrestling. It was a combination of many things, maturity and self-confidence being two major factors. But I still wasn't where I wanted to be, and, though probably unseen from the outside looking in, it was blatantly obvious to me. This is one of the few things I look back on in life and wish I could change. Instead of maintaining control of myself and my emotions, I had consciously allowed myself to be reactive and receptive to the natural feelings that were developing inside of me immediately following Don's death. I would allow my emotions to evolve and flow naturally. I was OK with being a passenger on this emotional rollercoaster. It was an overwhelming experience that I was dealing with, and maybe I hadn't quite evolved enough to handle the situation, but I denied one of the most fundamental principles of athletic success:

I should have stopped real life, focused 100% on the task at hand, and then resumed reality after the fight.

YOU control your mind; your mind doesn't control you. I should have stopped real life, focused 100% on the task at hand, and then resumed reality after the fight. Feeling how I felt was not wrong, but my mental state leading into competition was wrong. Once I made the decision to fight, I should have taken total control of myself, but I didn't. I went through the motions, but my mind was centered on Don. For the first few minutes of the fight,

I was on autopilot. Then maybe three minutes into the fight, reality set in. I was in the cage fighting Erik Silva, but I was thinking about Don. The dream scenario would have been to win gloriously, praise Don in the end, and then join family and friends to reflect on Don's life. However, the perfect dream doesn't just happen. You must MAKE IT HAPPEN.

There is a very important lesson to learn here, one that has showed its ugly face in my life on more than one occasion. I have no hesitation saying that I am a good person, though far from perfect. I do the right things. I train hard, treat people with respect, live with integrity. When I was younger, I used to think being a good person would naturally work in my favor, that in the ebb and flow of the world, the good people came out on top. And, since I was a good person, if I did my part, I would come out on top. I hadn't yet learned that the world can be brutally unfair. Good people do not always win. Sometimes very bad people win. Every act has a beginning and an end. And, while I do believe in fate, you must still perform your end of the deal. If it's your fate to be a star athlete or musician, you must spend your entire life working toward that fate. You can't just wait for it to happen, you must MAKE IT HAPPEN. As I did twice before in the state finals, I waited for my fate to come true. I forgot to MAKE IT HAPPEN. The beauty of bringing home the victory for Don would've played out nicely in a movie, and it

While I do believe in fate, you must still perform your end of the deal.

should have. But I stood in my own way from making that happen. I lost the fight via submission late in the first round.

Prior to flying home for Don's funeral, I stayed an extra night in Florida. I have always had an awesome support system throughout my life, and it continued into my fighting career. My close friends and family had made the trip to Florida, and a few of us decided to stay an extra night and enjoy ourselves. Don was constantly on my mind, but it was good to let go: cry, laugh, think. It was a nice escape.

When the weekend concluded, it was time to fly back to PA and face the situation. I had asked Don's family if I could speak at his funeral. Though I only knew him for a few years, I felt that I was well-suited to speak for a few reasons. Don and I had grown really close, and I was representing the work he was putting into mixed martial arts in the area. He was training several guys involved in MMA; it was a new, developing aspect of his career as a trainer. I planned out my speech with a few bullet points, but most of my speeches come from the heart. I could barely compose myself. Seeing everyone there, it was almost like a reunion from the gym. It was essentially the same people I'd see at No Limits, only we were dressed up and showing respect to the man who brought us all together.

I said many things about Don at his funeral—his selflessness, his addictively positive attitude, his enthusiasm for life, the constant energy that naturally rubbed off on every person he touched. I could've gone on forever. From my perspective, I was standing there as his best friend. But when I looked out over the crowd, I saw about a hundred of Don's other best friends. I realized at that moment that Don had an absolutely amazing ability to make you feel like his most prized, valuable friend in the entire world. He was so genuinely involved in his personal relationships that he made each one of us feel truly valued and appreciated. I left No Limits every day feeling that I had just spent an hour with my best friend, totally charged and ready to conquer the world. Every one of us felt the exact same way. It was then and there, standing in front of Don's disciples, that I realized he was a walking angel on earth.

Donald V. Messing passed away on June 7, 2012.

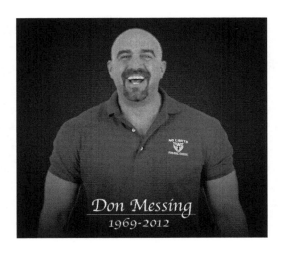

MOVING ON

Following Don's passing, there was no choice but to press on. I was left with a huge void in my training, so, once things settled a bit, I needed to address that situation. To be honest, Don was such an instrumental part of my routine that I felt a replacement would be somewhat of a dishonor to him. On top of that, there was absolutely no way anyone could meet the bar Don had set, not only as a strength coach, but also as a life coach. I decided to take a different approach to my strength training. I had been an athlete my entire life, so I decided to guide my own program. It'd been several years since I had gone to a normal gym to lift weights and train, so it was sort of refreshing. I used this period of time to get in the zone and really reflect on all of the things that Don had taught me. I knew so much more about strength training than I ever had, having spent two years picking Don's brain on a daily basis. After a few months of this routine, my brother Ben began to give his input on, and eventually guide, my strength training. He is a sounding board with everything I do, really, hence the moniker "ChAd." Whether it pertained to diet, fighting, or something so obscure as which pair of jeans to buy, I always asked him his opinion. Neither one of us is officially certified in strength and conditioning, but we have been training for over twenty years at a high level. Though we may not always know the exact science behind why something works, we do know what works. Ben and I had found a nice rhythm in our training, and he was assuming more of a hands–on approach to my career.

In September 2012, I lost my second consecutive fight in the UFC. I was released from the organization a few weeks later. I was 31 years old, just married, and my future was uncertain. The UFC is the biggest fighting organization in the world, and the basic structure of the MMA landscape is this: UFC, a few other major promotions, regional promotions, and lastly, local promotions. I was at a crossroads. Should I sign with another big organization, thus decreasing my chances of re-signing with the UFC in the foreseeable future, or should I fight on the regional and local circuits and hope I do enough to be re–signed? In addition, there was another big issue to address pertaining to my weight class. I had always fought at welterweight (170 lbs.), but my best bet to get back to the UFC was to drop a weight class and reinvent myself as a lightweight (155 lbs.). I had always been a

Although my opponents and I all weighed in at 170 pounds, they would come into the cage weighing between 185 and 200 pounds.

small welterweight, so the idea of dropping weight had followed me throughout my career. After some discussion with my team, we decided to drop to lightweight and take our chances on the regional circuit and work toward a return to the UFC. I was soon to be a lightweight fighter, and my sole goal was to get back to the UFC. I was determined to do whatever needed to be done.

The first step was a change in lifestyle that would enable me to make the 155 lb. weight class. While fighting at welterweight, I never really had to watch my diet. At times, I would actually try to consume as many calories as possible to gain weight. I was very undersized for the weight class, especially in the UFC. Although my opponents and I all weighed in at 170 pounds, they would come into the cage weighing between 185 and 200 pounds, no exaggeration. Because weigh-ins take place the day before the fight, there is plenty of time to refuel and put the weight back on. I normally entered the cage at 178 lbs. The drop in weight class needed to be done.

On the day I decided to do it, my work began. I cut out all unnecessary sugars and carbohydrates (Pepsi is my weakness), and I hit the road. Every day, I would run and run and run, burning all the calories I could, and this was in addition to my regular training regimen. I had considered getting a nutritionist to help lose the weight, but after 20+ years of wrestling and fighting, I knew my body as well as I knew anything. For me, losing weight and making weight, while not fun in the least, is a calculated, step-by-step process. I was so committed to making 155 lbs. that I weighed myself every morning and every night for months on end. I had certain goals each week, and, if I wasn't on pace to meet those goals, to the gym I went. To a nutrition specialist, perhaps my weight loss program could have been better in some ways, but it was perfect for me. I knew what my body could do.

Many times, when guys drop a weight class, they will do a test run to make sure their bodies can do it, as well as recover adequately for competition. Not everyone does one, but I thought it would be in my best interest. After all, there's no worse time to find out you can't recover well from the weight cut than in your first fight at the new weight. I would do my trial weight cut on a Thursday and train hard Friday, simulating the structure of fight week. The day before my trial weigh–in, I was 13 lbs. over the 156 lb. limit, fully hydrated. To some people, losing 13 pounds in 24 hours seems like lunacy, but it's actually very doable if you've prepared yourself in the preceding weeks and months. I did two workouts that day and woke up the next morning at 162 lbs., 6 lbs. over the lightweight limit (Unless it's a title fight, fighters receive a 1 lb. allowance). An hour and a half later, I weighed 155.8; I was now a lightweight. My next fight wasn't until the middle of January, but I wanted to make the cut in advance and simulate a fight the next day. This would give me a good gauge of the toll that the weight cut took on my body. When I went to bed that night, I weighed 172 lbs. The following day's training session was great, and there was no doubt I had found a home in my new weight class.

At this point in my career, I had experienced every level of the mixed martial arts spectrum. From fighting in small shows in my hometown, to co-headlining live on national TV in the UFC, I had taken quite a journey. But this was perhaps the toughest battle I was facing. My career had come full circle. I had a choice to make: call it quits and appreciate what I had done in my career, or start from scratch and dedicate myself to even further heights. It wasn't easy, having gone from such highs in the UFC to starting fresh on the local circuit, but I was committed to a goal, and I would do everything necessary to accomplish that goal.

My first fight after being released from the UFC was in front of my hometown fans in Altoona, PA. I won that fight via submission, and the tone was set for the remainder of the year. My self-confidence was at an all-time high, and my skills were improving rapidly. I had turned into a new type of fighter. Because I was so undersized at my previous weight class, it was difficult for me to finish fights. Looking back, I was so intent on keeping my opponents grounded in order to avoid their power on our feet that I often overlooked the concept of finishing fights. During 2013, however, I turned into a submission artist. I finished three of my four opponents by submission. It felt great. I was completely refreshed at lightweight, and I had found a great home in a growing regional promotion located in New Jersey, Cage Fury Fighting Championship

(CFFC). With the help of my manager, Mike, I was able to make a comfortable living while fighting close to home. It was all part of the process of getting back to the UFC.

By the end of May 2013, I had won two fights in my new weight class, but there were some bumps in the road in the following months. I had a fight scheduled for June, but up until eight days before the fight, I didn't know WHETHER I was fighting or WHOM I would be fighting. At such a critical spot in my career, I had to be

I've learned to expect the unexpected, because this industry is very fluid. Things change, people get hurt, and the sport attracts many unsavory people.

objective about accepting a fight with such flickering variables. We must have gone through five opponents before finally securing a fight. Thankfully, the fight went through, and I won. Then I was set to fight for the CFFC Lightweight Championship. This was a very big opportunity. We were thinking that a win here would put me back in contention to be re-signed with the UFC. And this fight would not be an easy one. My opponent was to be Kyle Baker, a tough, gritty, hard-nosed fighter who had been around for quite a while. He is the type of guy who fights just because he loves to fight. He had fought anywhere from 155 lbs. to 185 lbs. and had fought some of the toughest guys out there. Kyle and I had been on the same circuits off and on for several years, and he was one of those tough match ups that I knew would happen one day. The fight was scheduled for August.

In this sport, I've learned to expect the unexpected, because this industry is very fluid. Things change, people get hurt, and the sport attracts many unsavory people. I always tried to maintain a positive attitude, but I found it extremely difficult to really rely on anything, at least until it was actually happening. Three weeks prior to the fight, Baker had to pull out because of an injured shoulder. I had put up with a lot of heat from Kyle (personal jabs in the media), and now the fight was not going to happen. I took a deep breath, tried to ground myself, and looked to Mike to see what was next. After some shuffling, we were able to secure another opponent in time for the August 23 date. Thankfully, we could continue the course for my fourth fight of the year. It's very hard to consistently find fights for an ex–UFC fighter on the local/regional circuit, and I am extremely grateful to Mike and CFFC for making it happen.

While on site at the Borgata in Atlantic City, just when I thought everything was on course, it wasn't. During our ritual fight-day brunch with friends and family, as we were excitedly and nervously enjoying ourselves, Mike received a phone call from CFFC. They said my opponent had gotten sick the previous night after weigh-ins, and the fight was off. Just like that, my plans took a 180-degree turn. What can you do other than take a deep breath and accept it? Months of hard work flew out the window. After notifying all of my supporters who were making the trip to Atlantic City, it was back to the drawing board we went.

GRACIE JUNE

Amanda and I were expecting our first child in September of that year, so my immediate thought was to wait until after the baby was born to get back into fight training mode. Having a fight cancelled affects you in many ways. As I stated before, you've just put months of hard work into something that is not happening. Secondly, you have to consider the financial burden of not being paid. Sometimes, the promoters will give you your "show" money, but of course no "win" bonus. Many sponsors opt out of payment as well. More so, however, it's about the personal journey that comes along with preparing for, and then having, a professional fight. It's not just about the money.

Fighting is the purest way to release feelings within yourself. It draws out what you didn't even know existed. For months, you've accepted and come to grips with the fact that you will enter into a cage against another well-trained man and fight. On top of that, you have a logistical headache. Phone calls, ticket reimbursements—it's a big pain.

A few months after the debacle in August in Atlantic City, I was again scheduled to fight Kyle Baker for the CFFC Lightweight Championship. The fight was to take place in October, once again at the Borgata in Atlantic City. With the timing of our first child, I would have to be a bit creative when it came to completing my required workouts and meeting the requirements of a new father and husband. Right up to Gracie's birth, I was mostly living in New Jersey. I was still staying with Jackie during the week and commuting home on the weekends. For chunks of five days at a time, I would be away from Amanda during her pregnancy. She was staying at home alone, and that was difficult for me to endure. If something had happened to her or the baby, I would never have been able to forgive myself. But Amanda knew how tough Kyle was, and she understood that it was for the best that I was in New Jersey.

Sometimes, life isn't black and white. You can love two things at the same time that don't fit nicely together. For me to maximize myself as a fighter, I felt I had to be in New Jersey. At the same time, there is nothing more I wanted than to be at home with Amanda. I couldn't do both, and she supported me in my journey. During this time away, my in-laws really took over. We are so fortunate to have them nearby. Amanda was never alone. They were making up for my absence. I actually worried that some of her family might see me as selfish for being away. Like I said before, sometimes things don't add up. 2+2 isn't always 4. Yes, I was away from my pregnant wife so I could train. But by training in New Jersey I'd become the best fighter I could be, and all of the things I wanted for my wife and soon-to-appear daughter could be made possible. To me, to us, it made sense. I've come to learn that that's all that matters. Amanda was being taken care of in my absence by our family and friends, and I'm very thankful for their help. I also made it a point to go to every doctor's appointment with her during the pregnancy, save one. This was really the first time in my life that I had to mix my professional and personal lives. Before, I could come and go as I pleased, letting Amanda know when and where I would be. Now, life was changing. It was no longer about me, it was about our family.

At 6 AM on September 24, I received an early-morning phone call while I slept peacefully in New Jersey. "I think my water broke." I blurted, "You 'think' you're water broke, or it broke?!" I was in a very interesting situation here. As a husband and soon-to-be father, it was obviously my number one priority to be with Amanda during her pregnancy. But at the same time, we needed to be sure she was going into labor before I made the two-and-a-half hour trip home. However, had I missed the birth of our first child because of training, now THAT would have been bad news. A few minutes later, Amanda called me back and said there was no doubt she was going into labor. Luckily and coincidentally, her best friend, also named Amanda, had stayed over the night before, so the two of them began the process of heading to the hospital. I immediately jumped out of bed, prepared my morning tea (a daily ritual) and hit the road for PA.

I was already your typical glowing dad, smiling from ear to ear, singing along to every song on the radio and most likely speeding along Route 78. We ironically arrived at the Harrisburg hospital within minutes of each other. The nurse had Amanda wait a while before leaving for the hospital. I was very tired from the early morning drive, so as soon as we got settled in our room, I sprawled out on the cold, concrete floor. Amanda began to chuckle to herself. Little did I know this was our actual delivery room, and that this floor had played host to many deliveries and things that come along with delivering a baby (If you've been there, you know). I was comfortably sprawled out, soaking up the experience, clueless to it all. We were in for a long day, and I was already asking permission to get my workouts in for the day. I had enough contacts in the area that I could organize a few unscheduled workouts over the next few days. I was treading on thin ice—performing my duties as a husband and father, but not foregoing my professional commitment as a fighter. If this were any other profession, a few days off would be just that, but fighting is a different type of profession. A few days off doesn't just mean putting in extra hours to make up for lost time. You've LOST that time, and that could have very serious repercussions.

The next few days were a blur. I have never been so tired in my life, and this was a good preview of what was to come as a father. I remember at one point sleeping with my eyes wide open. It was intense, but watching this process was the most amazing thing I had ever experienced.

My wife gave birth to our first child, Gracie June Brenneman, on September 24, 2013. Everyone, including myself, had thought we were having a boy (we didn't find out ahead of time). All of the old wives' tales pointed toward a boy, so when a girl emerged, we were both quite surprised but incredibly happy. We had created two plans of action depending on whether it was a boy or a girl. Since it was a girl, and our girl's name was Gracie, I threw on one of my Gracie Jiu-Jitsu shirts before I went out to get my family, discreetly sharing that we had a little girl. (Amanda actually picked the name. Coincidentally, it's a great name to share in the professional fighting world. The Gracie family is one of the most famous names in MMA and jiu jitsu).

Though we had kept the baby names private, my mother-in-law actually caught the little hint, but it was quickly passed over when my mom suggested it was just one of my "fighting shirts." Our families got to meet little Gracie June, and everyone immediately fell in love. My parents, though, were already planning their departure. 120 miles away, Ben's wife, Meghan, was also in labor. We couldn't have planned it if we had tried. I'll note that this is one of the only times Ben has ever lied to me. When Amanda and I shared the pregnancy news with everyone, Ben and Meghan were a bit off in their reaction; something was wrong. I called him on it directly, as we always do with each other, and he assured me that nothing was wrong, and they were extremely happy for us.

Weeks later, I stumbled upon prenatal vitamins at their apartment. Of course, I asked, and he assured me she wasn't pregnant, another lie. Tsk, tsk, ChAd! Obviously she was, and it was awesome. My parents left for Stroudsburg and were able to meet Gracie's cousin, Wilson Marie, the next day, September 25. Gracie and Willa are 21 hours apart. I was hoping for "twin cousins," and as I (half) jokingly asked Amanda to stay strong until midnight (Gracie was born at 11:06 PM), I was sternly reminded by all of the women in the room, as politely as possible, to shut my mouth.

I was sternly reminded by all of the women in the room, as politely as possible, to shut my mouth.

After Gracie's birth, I stayed at home for a few days before heading back to Jersey to resume training. Truth be told, I would have stayed home much longer if I hadn't had Amanda's support 100%. I felt bad on many levels leaving Gracie and her, but that was the reality of our situation. I felt very comfortable knowing that Amanda and Gracie were at home with family and friends by their side. This was the first time that, as a man, I saw just how much mothers do for their children. I am a very, very involved father. From changing diapers to feeding, I do it all. BUT what Amanda does as a mother far surpasses what I do as a father. It's remarkable. One of the most important lessons I will pass on to Gracie is that she will ALWAYS show respect for her mother, and one day she will realize why. Mothers do for their children what no one else can do. I saw firsthand the unbreakable bond that exists between mother and child. It made me sit back and realize just how much my mom has done for me in my lifetime, not just the times I can remember but since the day I was born. That old saying, "Wait until you have a child of your own—then you'll understand"—it rings true in countless ways.

BACK TO FIGHTING

I t was now time to get back in the cage, and October 26, 2013, was one of the most memorable nights in my professional fighting career. I was finally set to fight Kyle Baker for the CFFC Lightweight Championship, and the fight went as perfectly as planned. I was able to use my dominant wrestling game and improved striking to control the entire fight. It was one of my best performances inside the cage. In the back of my mind, Kyle had been a potentially tough opponent for five years, so this was a personal victory as well as a professional one. Everything just clicked during the fight. My corner men did an excellent job, and my body was on autopilot; I was able to finish the fight with a second round submission. This would hopefully be enough to get me back to the UFC. I had won four fights so far in the year, three of them by submission, and the right people were starting to notice. I did my part inside the cage, and Mike went to work outside the cage, keeping the UFC updated on my progress. I was done fighting for 2013, and Amanda, Gracie and I were able to enjoy our new family back home in Middletown, PA. The new year would be brought in with great news.

BACK TO THE UFC!

The call couldn't have come at a better time. I was ringing in the new year with a bang. No sooner had I finished my second helping of pork and sauerkraut (a tasty Central PA good-luck tradition) than the phone rang. It was Mike. I was back in the UFC. The fight was to take place in Atlanta, GA on January 14, exactly two weeks later. I had been training here and there over the holidays, but I was surely not in fight mode. I had worked so hard to get back to the UFC, and there was no way I was going to let this opportunity pass by. Fast-forward two weeks, and it was over as quickly as it began. That's the thing about fighting—all the cheery, good feelings either come to a crashing halt or intensify exponentially immediately after the fight. There is no in-between. Winning or losing an individual fight has a profound impact on your career. It seemed like I was back in my living room before I even left for Georgia, as if it never even happened. OK, so let's take a mulligan on that one. Short-notice fight, right after the holidays, let's regroup and get this next one. But before I get on to the next one, let me explain where I was at internally at this time.

MMA had been good to me up to this point, but I had also let it affect me in a negative way. Little by little over the years, I had become jaded. I was increasingly sick of the ugly side of the business. Professional sports, I thought, were supposed to be professional. MMA, in many ways, is the exact opposite. Some people in the sport are completely unqualified to be doing what they are doing— some promoters, managers, trainers, and even fighters. On top of that, the next big thing is always just around the corner. It can be a game of empty promises and occasional follow-throughs. If I were to add up all of the "next big things" in my career, I'd be a quadrillionaire. We are constantly waiting on "the next call." When you sign a contract, you can only HOPE it is fulfilled by the other side. Many deals are just handshakes, and if there is an actual contract, it's nothing more than a flimsy piece of paper. Sometimes, it has no meaning. Fighters are as

MMA had been good to me up to this point, but I had also let it affect me in a negative way. Little by little over the years, I had become jaded.

bad as anyone in not fulfilling contracts. Guys come in overweight, or they don't show up at all for a contracted fight. Some sponsors choose not to pay, even after the fighters complete their end of the bargain. I'm still owed $2100 that I will never receive, and I consider myself lucky that it's only $2100. To this day, there are stories of some of the biggest promotions in the world not paying their fighters. I could go on forever, and maybe someday I will, but for now—you get the gist of what I'm saying.

Regardless, I was allowing myself to focus on the negatives of others rather than focusing on what I had the power to control. I was letting these external factors, ones that were beyond my influence, affect me as a person. I was irritable and negative. I had convinced myself that my way of thinking must be the right way because it's what I thought, and only I had experienced MY life situation. I would later come to realize that my current life situation was not much different from everyone else's. I just happened to be a professional fighter. We all have problems, whether it's an unqualified boss or an undeserving colleague who gets a promotion. I was just being sensitive, and it was having a negative effect on me as a person and a fighter. Don't get me wrong, I was happy with life in general, but my professional life was taking its toll on me. Those closest to me could see my negativity, but with what I thought was 20/20 perspective, I saw none of it.

Around that time, the winter of 2014, I was in the process of transitioning my training from NJ/NY to Philadelphia. I had had enough of living on the road. I wanted to be with my family, and I felt I could do both—train at the highest level AND be with my family. Amanda put no pressure on me to make this move. It was my decision. It just got to a point where I couldn't do it anymore. I was driving 15-20 hours a week, and my training was beginning to deteriorate. I was depending on people who couldn't be depended on. Sessions were being cancelled, and guys were not showing up as consistently as they had been. Things were changing. It was no one's fault. It was just evolution. The years of driving hours-on-end for training were catching up to me. It was the price I paid for surrounding myself with the best. Some guys had it better than I did, and some guys had it worse. The reality of my situation is that the level of MMA is higher in surrounding states than in PA. I could either up and move, or I could spend a great deal of time on the road. I chose the latter, and I have no regrets. New Jersey had been absolutely amazing to me in countless ways. Everyone there had welcomed me into their homes and gyms and helped me concentrate on becoming the best fighter I could be. But now it was time to familiarize myself with the City of Brotherly Love.

A TRANSITION

Part of the reason I love living in Middletown is its central location and the ease of travel into and out of town. Philadelphia is a 90-minute train ride from Middletown, and the train station is a one-minute (okay, maybe two-minute) drive from my home. Amanda grew up in Middletown, just outside of Harrisburg, and it served as a great place to start our lives together. We were around family and friends, and I was able to get high-level training within a two-hour drive or train ride. When I made the decision to transition my training to Philly, the ease of travel was a very big component, as I was trying to improve my quality of life. More importantly, though, was the quality of training in the city. I had a great deal of contacts over the years of fighting, so I made some calls and got busy training. Balance Studios welcomed me in with open arms. I had met the owners, brothers

Phil and Ricardo Migliarese, years earlier, and they were happy to assist me in any way they could. It was nice, new, and fresh, and I was 25 fights into my career. The change was a bit scary, too. I'm not going to sugar coat it, either. Ben and I had some serious discussions about whether or not this was the right decision. In his mind, it was not. In his opinion, such a drastic change this late in a career was not a good idea. But what I knew was that I could no longer continue at the pace I was going. Life is a shifting mix of all components involved. In my opinion, for true success and happiness, you must achieve a perfect balance. So while my professional life in New Jersey was maxed out in efficiency and output (until recently), my personal life was not. My relationship with Amanda was fine, but all the little things that went along with traveling

All the little things that went along with traveling so much were wearing me down. At times, I felt like a walking zombie.

so much were wearing me down. At times, I felt like a walking zombie. I couldn't commit to anything because I never knew where I was going to be. In all, I wouldn't have made the move if I didn't think I could continue to train at the level I needed to in order to compete in the UFC. Fighting is not just something fun that you do, at least not for me. I had always been all in, or I would have gotten out. This was a profession to me, not a hobby or a game. My entire professional life, and personal life for that matter, was based around fighting and training. Every ounce of my energy went into becoming a better fighter. And though the environment was changing, the process and end goal were the same.

After training for a few months in Philly, I was given my next fight by the UFC. Things were going well in training. I was doing most of it in Philly at Balance, but I'd make a weekly trip to either New Jersey or upstate New York to connect with my training partners and BJJ coach Brian McLaughlin. It was a nice mix; training was intense and fulfilling, AND I was able to sleep at home most nights of the week. Looking back on this period of time, I can see some misalignment in my life. My brother and I had some friction based on our views of such a drastic change in training so late in my career. There was also no continuity among my head trainers. Everyone was located in a different state, and, although I was in sync with each individual coach, there was not an overall connection amongst us. There was no ill-will or negativity; it was just logistically impossible to spend time together as a group.

LIGHTS OUT IN BALTIMORE

April 26, 2014, saw me fight Danny Castillo at UFC 172 in Baltimore, Maryland. It was a 90-minute drive from my home, and my friends and family were able to make the trip. Everything leading up to the fight was great. I was confident in my training and preparation. This fight was meant to be, just not for the reason I had thought. I won the first round, but Castillo and his team had done their homework. I had gotten into a bad habit of reaching out a lazy jab, most often for no apparent reason. I wasn't gauging distance or setting up my opponent for another shot. I was just doing it, a practice I would really dive into transforming following this fight. Though my brother is not a fighter or an official coach, he has a gift for observing and noting my technical mistakes (and boy is he good at it). He had mentioned my lazy jab often leading up to the fight, but I didn't correct it. Let me be totally honest here. Because Ben is my brother and because he is not a professional fighter, I sometimes discarded what he said. At this point in our relationship, I probably did it more than ever. And it cost me. It was the first time I had ever been knocked unconscious. I had been hit hard in my career but never actually been out of it in a fight. If I got dropped, I got right back up or positioned myself accordingly. (You can see what I mean in my fights against Johny Hendricks and Anthony Johnson). My only point here is that getting knocked out was a completely new and extremely scary experience to me. Danny connected with an overhand right just as I reached out my lazy jab. It was a one–punch knockout. I fell backward and was immediately out. In a very quick, split–second decision, Danny refrained from hitting me as I was unconscious on the ground. It happened so quickly that the ref had to sprint to Danny to stop the fight. In that time, he could have unloaded a few more hard shots to my unconscious self. I'm grateful to him that he didn't. It's a strong sign of sportsmanship.

The aftermath was rough, in so many ways. Physically, I felt fine for a few hours, but then developed a headache. The vision in my left eye began to succumb to the aura sensation of a migraine. For the next day or two, I was more or less okay, except for vision trouble coming and going. On the Tuesday after my fight, however, I couldn't get out of bed. I had a severe headache that kept me immobilized and in bed all day. I had just gotten knocked out on live national television. My parents, wife, siblings, aunts, uncles, friends, fans, haters—everyone saw it. My emotional state was as low as it had ever been, except for my second state final loss. I was stuck in bed with a headache from HELL; my sweet in-laws had to watch their daughter's husband who fights for a living lie in bed unable to care for his daughter. And, to top it off, I was getting the most ruthless hate mail and social media comments you could imagine. What evil things could you possibly say to a guy who just put it all on the line and got knocked out in front of the world? You'd be amazed. I was fragile and internally destroyed. In hindsight, this was a very valuable learning experience, but at the time, I would have done anything to forget it all.

I was getting the most ruthless hate mail and social media comments you could imagine.

I requested brain imaging to make sure I was okay. The initial scans showed bruising, which according to medical experts was not out of the ordinary following a concussion, but the prognosis was positive. I had to get another scan done eight weeks later to make sure that I healed as expected. I was extremely careful during this time. Concussions and brain trauma had recently become the hot topic in professional sports, so it was on my mind every second of the day. I did absolutely nothing for a month, and then I eased into cardio. I wouldn't spar for another few months following my second scan. I think this is why I've been successful thus far in my life. I take the extra step in whatever I do. Tell me to wait two months to spar after a concussion, and I'll wait four. Tell me to save six months' worth of living expenses in the bank, I'll save a year's worth. Tell me to drill something 100 times, I'll do it 500. If there is one thing I am, it's obsessive. The scans came back normal, and I was medically cleared to resume fighting. However, I wasn't totally sure that was the road I would take.

TO FIGHT OR NOT TO FIGHT?

Immediately began to question my future in the sport. I basically decided that I was done—an emotional decision, I see now in retrospect. Amanda wanted me to be done, and my brother initially agreed. My parents toggled between my happiness and my health. It was a tough time. Mike was up in the air. He always has a sense of control in any situation, and when I said that I didn't know what to do, he responded, "You don't have to make a decision right now. Sit on it." And that's exactly what I did.

Sitting for that month following my knockout nearly drove me crazy. I was able to stay at home with Gracie every day, which was amazing, but there was another part of me that needed a purpose. Months earlier, prior to my Castillo fight, I had received a message from Justin Greskiewicz, a professional muay thai fighter (similar to kickboxing) in Philadlephia who was interested in working with me. Up to this point, I had had several striking coaches in my career. I had learned a great deal over the years, but the one thing I lacked was consistency. I was able to have a certain amount of consistency for chunks of time, but then for one reason or another, that would change. I get along with each of my former coaches, but life would continually get in the way. Another unfortunate truth of this sport is that it is a business, and it costs money, a lot of it. Private one-on-one sessions with a coach can cost upward of $100 per hour. Multiply that by twice a week, and the numbers start to get daunting. I make decent money fighting, but on top of all the other expenses, it can be tough to keep up. I wanted more, but I just couldn't swing it. Enter Justin.

On May 30, 2014, I started what would become one of the most valuable relationships I've formed in MMA. Justin has had over 60 fights and has fought the best of the best. We immediately clicked. I had identified a few areas of my game that needed to be addressed, and unless I fixed them, I didn't want to continue fighting. It had occurred to me after the Castillo fight that my vision—not my actual perception, but rather where my eyes look during a fight—was way off. The truth is that I had no idea where I looked. I would

A few areas of my game needed to be addressed, and unless I fixed them, I didn't want to continue fighting.

just see a thing in front of me. I had always been amazed at boxers' ability to slip punches. Aha! It was because they were looking at the punches as they were coming. It was an epiphany. I was an idiot. No wonder the only times I really got hit were solid, hard punches that seemingly came from left field. It's because I had no idea where they were coming from. I wasn't looking in the right place. I passed this on to Justin, and we went to work.

To get to Philly, as I had mentioned, I took the train to center city. From there, Justin's gym was a 25-minute subway ride or a $15 cab ride away. What Justin did for me over the next six months and beyond was supremely generous and selfless. He would pick me up in the morning, train me prior to class, help me during class, and then bring me back to the train station after class. And I wasn't making him rich. He valued and appreciated the work I was putting in. And for the first time in a very long time, I was able to train in striking nearly every day. The only hiccup was getting over to Philly. But, if I was able to get there, he would make time for me. We went at this pace for six months before my next fight. He not only became a trainer, he became a close friend.

On the other side of the coin, I had continued to train with Brian in BJJ. I would do some of my BJJ training in Philly, but I would meet up with Brian and some of my old training partners once a week in New Jersey. Brian has always been an unbelievably giving coach and friend. One time, he actually paid for his own airfare to Japan to corner one of our teammates. He sees the big picture in everything that he does. We had developed an MMA/BJJ session on Wednesdays over in New Jersey, so I'd make the three-hour trip over, train, then make the three-hour trip home. It was tough, but it was worth it.

I still didn't even know whether I was going to fight again, I just knew that if I did, I was going to be very well–prepared. I had made a decision after the Castillo fight: Unless I noticed a significant improvement in my abilities as a fighter, I was not going to compete anymore. It was not worth getting in there and risking my health if I was not capable of being the best Spaniard that ever was. It's a scary part of being a professional athlete. We all decline. It's nature, and fighting is something you want to exit too soon rather than too late. After two lousy performances, I needed to be certain that my abilities weren't declining.

Something else in me changed as well after the Castillo fight. I was shaken with the mortality of being a fighter. Never before had I imagined being done. It scared me. I had absolutely no idea what I wanted to do next. I had two degrees and wasn't totally opposed to going back to teaching or pursuing Spanish in another industry, but I have an inner desire to do something extraordinary with my life. It's hard to pinpoint exactly what it is, but it is centered on helping other people fulfill their potential as human beings. I see too

I was shaken with the mortality of being a fighter. Never before had I imagined being done.

many kids walking around with no self–confidence and too many adults stuck in a job in which they don't want to be. I just want to be me and share what I've learned on my journey so that it can inspire people to take action in their own lives. The scary reality, though, is that I have a family and a mortgage and a car and my desire to help others does not pay the bills. Not yet! So I set out on a mission to learn as much as I could about personal development, about being the best person I could possibly be, so I could then help others. I began reading as much as I could and listening to as many motivating and inspiring podcasts and interviews as possible. I started to write down some of my ideas in hope of some clarification. My morning routine shifted from drinking tea and surfing the Internet for 30 minutes, to waking up before Gracie and reading valuable books (I'm not perfect, I must add. I still waste time. Just much, much less). My commutes to Philly and New Jersey turned into opportunities to listen and learn rather than a daunting day on the road. I was introduced to new people and picked their brains on business. I wanted to learn as much as I could ... about everything. I'd never been a "business" guy. I had always been bad at sales and negotiation, as evidenced earlier by my T-shirt-refund-for-no-reason example. Talking money has always made me feel uncomfortable. I was as new to the personal development arena as I once was to fighting. But just as I dove right into fighting, I dove right into this new world. The fact that my fighting days were limited created in me a drive to figure out what's next in my life.

UBERLANDIA

I had been training intensely from June until my next fight in November. I really and truly believe these were some of the most valuable months of my career. Justin and I had gotten into a groove with my striking training and sparring, my BJJ and ground work was as good as ever between Balance and Brian, and my strength and conditioning had been rejuvenated as well. I had been working consistently with Tim Pollock, a personal trainer close to my home in Middletown. Amanda and I had driven past his studio a thousand times, each time thinking how similar it was to Don's studio back in East Stroudsburg. It was a sign. One day I stopped in, and we clicked. Tim and I had spent five months of intense training together. I was at the peak of my conditioning in every way possible. In addition, I had started working with a sports psychologist. I had covered all bases leading into this next fight. Mentally, physically, psychologically—I was operating at a ten. No longer was I irritated by the business or other uncontrollable factors in my life and career. My training was going great, and I had improved my quality of life greatly. Just six months earlier, I was contemplating retiring from MMA, but now I felt as prepared as ever heading into a fight.

"Uber what?" I asked when Mike told me I'd be fighting in Brazil. Uberlandia, Brazil is a small town in southeast Brazil that would play host to Ultimate Fight Night 56 on November 8, 2014. If it would have been at any other time in my career, I probably would have dreaded the trip, and here is why. There are some outside factors that had created in me a negative opinion of fighting down in Brazil. It has nothing to do with being in "enemy" territory (I was fighting a Brazilian). When you fight internationally, you are subject to that country's taxes, which means less money in your pocket. With many countries, you are given a tax credit with the U.S. at tax time, but in my experiences, it doesn't benefit the fighter to fight out of country. Secondly, I was concerned about the travel itself. Fighters are accustomed to certain foods and protocols during fight week. It is much easier to adhere to these procedures at home on U.S. soil rather than in a country to which I've never been. And, lastly, I had to cover the flights of two of my cornermen. The UFC covers one corner flight; it is up to the fighter to cover the other two. Two flights to Brazil were $4,000, and with a purse of $10K/$10K (show/ win bonus) for this fight, $4,000 was a significant portion. Prior to my initial release from the UFC in 2012, I was making

$18K/$18K for my fights. However, when I re-signed on short notice in 2014, I was brought back down to $10K/$10K. Unless you are a champion or unique individual, there is generally no bargaining power with the UFC. It was a much better offer than I was getting on the regional level, so we took it. Having lost my previous two fights, my pay had not increased. So as you can see, a few bad fights can have a dramatic effect on your lifestyle. Thankfully, some generous sponsors helped me cover a good portion of the cost of the flights. More importantly, I was ready to fight.

The week in Brazil was great. It was my brother Ben; my two trainers, Brian and Justin; and me. Despite Brian's trip from hell, which saw him fly all over the country before finally arriving in Uberlandia, it was all positive energy. As the fighter, you are responsible for putting your corner men up in hotel rooms for the week, as well as covering their meals. When you're fighting for $10K–$20K, it adds up. Brazil was fighter–friendly, as a U.S. dollar converted quite well to a Brazilian real (Brazil's currency). So an added bonus was that there was no financial burden on me. Every sign we saw was pointing in the right direction, a Spaniard victory.

It was like I had tunnel vision. All I saw was what was in front of me, and that was Leandro Silva. I had studied his fights. We knew his tendencies. This was a fight that I wanted, one that I thought for sure I would win. The Brazilian crowd is one of the most intense crowds you can face. The arena was small and intimate. There were about 6000 fans, all rooting for their Brazilian fighter. But to be honest, I barely heard them.

I was totally focused. One thing I had learned from my sports psychology sessions was the idea of Positive Cognitive Reframing, or turning your negative perspective into a positive one. I looked at this as an opportunity to shine in an unfavorable situation, just like Rocky did against the Russian. (Though Rocky can be a bit cliché, I find myself referring to those movies in very pivotal moments of my life).

My mantra of "footprints and vision," something I had picked up to help keep me centered on the task in front of me, reminded me to stay focused and moving, my eyes centered directly below my opponent's chin, and my feet never staying in one place. This was one of the things I had worked on diligently with Justin over the previous six months, staying focused

I looked at this as an opportunity to shine in an unfavorable situation, just like Rocky did against the Russian.

and present, never letting my eyes shift from their intended target, and always moving with purpose. These were two aspects of fighting that, after 26 professional fights, I finally understood. The reason that when I got hit, I got hit hard and often dropped was that I never saw the punches coming. My movements, while on my feet, were erroneous and had no purpose; I was just moving for the sake of moving. It sounds basic and obvious, but it was also a powerful realization that I'm glad came late rather than never. As soon as the fight began, I knew I felt different. My abilities to gauge distance and stay in the pocket were immediate clues of my improvement. I had always felt far away from my opponent in my fights, though I always felt comfortable with my distance in practice. I attribute this to my previous mental and emotional states in my earlier fights. I had always operated with a "full throttle" mindset, never allowing the natural ebb and flow of a fight to come through. I was either all in or all out. Training was a much more relaxed setting. Though intense, I was not in the fire during practice. During an actual fight, it was much different. For a majority of my fights, the full throttle mindset worked, but against the best, I needed to add a sense of calm to the mix.

For the first four minutes of the fight, I was everything I had trained to be. I wasn't perfect, but I was really good, and I was controlling the fight. I was able to out-strike Leandro, and my takedowns were on. I was surprised at his strength, but it wasn't enough to prevent me from putting him on the mat. It was all falling into place, but just like that, it came to a screeching halt. The one major area of concern with this fight was my opponent's ability to "take the back" of his opponent. This is when your opponent is able to position himself behind you, controlling your body with his arms and legs; it leaves you open to a "rear naked choke," basically a strangle hold. Brian had reiterated a thousand times, "Whatever you do, do not let him take your back." Well, in a scramble, I did allow him to take my back. As I had mentioned, Leandro was stronger than I had expected. He also had better hips than anticipated. Once he took my back, he pounced immediately. It was as if his choke attempt went from intention to 100% locked-in position in a split second. Normally when someone attempts to choke you, it's a gradual process. You feel the choke being initiated, you begin to fight, and there is a back-and-forth jockeying for position. I just remember thinking, "The choke is coming," and reaching down to peel one of his hooks (reposition one of his legs)—but the choke was already in. I reached up to try to peel one of his hands, but I couldn't reach it. The choke was in securely and deeply. One of the techniques you learn through training is to use the old "poker face" when being choked. Your opponent could be squeezing with all of his power, but if you remain calm and convey that

All I could think of was my mom having to see me unconscious again on TV.

you are unaffected, he will often release the technique to reposition or conserve his energy. I attempted this, but it was too tight. I distinctly remember it being hot in the cage that night. Within a second or two, the walls began to close in around me, and my consciousness was fading. All I could think of was my mom having to see me unconscious again on TV, so I consciously made the decision to tap. Some fighters proclaim proudly that they'll never tap, that it's a sign of weakness. Call me weak if you want. Proving my toughness to anyone is far less important than making the right decision for my family.

And, just like that, it was over. It wasn't supposed to end like this. I had done everything in my power to come home with a victory. I had done everything I could for the last 25 years to get this victory. I was empty. Defeat, whether you think you are prepared for it or not, is never easy. No matter how much work you put into improving and staying positive, there is always, always, an initial period of time following defeat in which nothing anyone could ever say would make any difference. There is only one thing that helps, and that is time.

I had done everything correctly, and I still lost that fight. It took months for me to realize the positives that came from the previous eight months of life and training that had led me to Brazil.

REFLECTION

When I look back at my competitive life, which has spanned 25 years, there is one constant that has never faltered in any way, and that is my family. I have had their support from the first day I stepped on the wrestling mat at the age of eight, and I am confident I will have their support in anything I choose to do for the rest of my life. This extends from my immediate and extended families all the way to my new family with Amanda and Gracie. We are comfortably middle-class, but in my eyes, we are wealthy. Scott, Nicki, Ben and I were raised in a traditional family environment. We were surrounded by family on a daily basis. We were always together celebrating something. My friends would often joke that "the Brennemans have a party for everything." It is a bit comical if you look at it from an outside perspective, but it's perfectly normal to us. My mom still bakes us birthday cakes and makes us special birthday meals. Family helped shape us into the people we are today. We aren't perfect by any means, and we have our share of conflict, but the overall picture is one of support and love. I thank God every day for my family and the blessings we have together.

Ocean City, MD pic, 2015.
Brenneman family tradition.

My parents, Charles "Butch" and Marie Brenneman, have done more for us than we could have ever asked. We have had their love and support from Day One. While their backgrounds are extremely different, my parents came together to produce a great family and marriage. My mom comes from a strong Italian background, while my dad spent his youth growing up on the farm. The two sides of my family are so different, and as an adult, I have come to deeply appreciate both sides. On one hand, we were raised on homemade pasta and an abundance of hugs and kisses. On the other, we were privy to a small community that was based on waking up early in the morning and spending all day on the farm. On paper, my parents had regular jobs and a regular house, but in reality, they are much more. They have raised four kids to become four successful adults with a strong set of moral values and sense of family. Scott, Nicki, Ben and I are lucky that this Italian Catholic from Altoona and this hardworking farmer from Hollidaysburg met that night many years ago at Louie's Coral Lounge, a local hotspot back in the day.

Growing up, I had no concept of money. That's an odd statement, so let me explain. We were middle–class all the way, but I didn't want for anything. I can't think of one thing I wanted as a child that my parents didn't provide. Please don't misinterpret that—I was certainly not spoiled. My parents believed that if we did our best in school and in life, they would help us as much as they could along the way. Growing up, I was exposed to many prominent families in my area, but I never ever felt like I didn't belong. It all came back to my parents. They gave everything, and more, to us kids. I think back to how many out-of-state trips they took in my wrestling career, the new skis, computers, cell phones, all of it. My parents made the most with what they had so their kids could be happy. "I shop at

It all came back to my parents. They gave everything, and more.

Kmart," my mom said, "so you can shop at the Gap." As an adult with a child of my own, I see the value of how they raised us and the effort it took. My goal is to provide for my family just as my parents did for us.

When I began fighting, my parents didn't know how to feel. They were concerned for my safety and would've preferred that I had chosen another profession to pursue. However, for better or worse, I am the type of person who, once I make up my mind on something, it is very hard to change my view. I wanted to become a professional fighter. My parents saw this authentic desire and decided to support me in my quest. And, not only did I have my parents' support, I had my entire family behind me. They traveled across the country to support me in my fights—California, Texas, North Carolina, Atlanta—they were there. Parents, siblings, aunts, uncles, cousins—they all made the trips to show their support. My Godparents, Carol Jo and Allen, have been traveling around the country with me since I was an eight-year-old wrestler. They all went the extra mile to show their support in everything throughout my career.

I vividly remember standing just outside the park entrance, inconsolable, wanting to throw my medal deep into the darkness.

One of the most memorable moments in my life happened in 1999, just after I lost in the state finals for the second year in a row. At that time, it was the most heartbreaking thing that could've happened. I was SUPPOSED to win states my senior year, but I just didn't MAKE IT HAPPEN. Immediately after the match, I held myself together just long enough to get outside the Hershey Park Arena. I vividly remember standing just outside the park entrance, inconsolable, wanting to throw my medal deep into the darkness of the park. I was surrounded by family. I believe it was my oldest brother, Scott, who was holding me upright. I had nothing left. My world had gone, but I was surrounded by the people who loved me most. That moment was symbolic in that, no matter what, my family would be there to pick me up. As I look back on that moment, and all of those wrestling and fighting moments of heartbreak and disappointment, I realize that they have helped to shape me into the man I am today, and I can genuinely say that I wouldn't change a thing.

As we continue to grow and create our own lives, the Brenneman "kids" continue to be linked. Scott is a lawyer. Nicki is an English teacher. Ben is a high school administrator. And I am me, still in the process of figuring that out. But as we ebb and flow in our own lives, we never lose touch of one another. Not long ago, I was on a training trip with one of my coaches. My cell phone kept buzzing from a group text message that had been going on for months. I apologized to him and explained the situation that my siblings and I have a group message that is nonstop at times. He was genuinely surprised and commented on how neat it was that we were so close. To me, it was just another text in a thousand-message strand. But when I sat back and realized just how uncommon that is in today's world, I just smiled to myself. Ma and Pa, you did an awesome job of raising us.

As a competitor, losing is never easy and the losses continue to nag at you well into the future, but learning and improving from setbacks is the key to success. Some of the most successful people in the world have had countless numbers of setbacks in their lives as well. But, they just don't take no for an answer. For many years, I've rolled with the setbacks and remained resolute in overcoming them, and in the latter portion of my career, I've shifted my focus. For as long as I can remember, my focus was simply on becoming the best: the best wrestler in the state, the best wrestler in the country, the best fighter in the world. But, now, I focus everyday on becoming the best ME that I can possibly be. I'm a firm believer in maximizing YOUR abilities to the max, no matter what those abilities are. Do that, and the rest will fall into place. I do my best to concentrate my energy on myself; it's a lot less stressful than worrying about my competition. So here I am, sitting on my couch, ten days after my last fight, trying to figure out what's next in my life. I might be done fighting, my career with the UFC is most likely done forever, and I end this story just as I began it, asking myself, "How can I make a life in which I am personally and financially free?" I'm not completely sure, but no matter how I am remembered as a fighter, I have personal satisfaction in knowing that I once sat in my classroom at the Hollidaysburg Area Junior High School and thought, "Wouldn't it be cool to be a UFC fighter?"

Extras/Afterword

MY RUN–IN WITH BONES

I was scheduled to fight in Las Vegas in September 2012. As a fighter, fighting in Las Vegas is a big deal. It's the fight capital of the world. After 20 or so fights, I had yet to experience a fight in Las Vegas. It was all set ... until it wasn't. I had just finished a wrestling session at Edge Wrestling in Hoboken, New Jersey, when I showered up and grabbed my phone. When I see missed calls from Mike and Ben at the same time, it's a sign that something is amiss. On top of that, the first text message I read was something like, "I'm so sorry man." I called Mike, and he gave me the news. One of the main event fighters had gotten injured. The promoters had proposed that the other fighter, Jon Jones (the UFC Light Heavyweight

Champion) fight Chael Sonnen. Jon turned down the fight, and the entire event was subsequently cancelled. I was no longer going to Vegas. This was the first time in UFC history that an event was cancelled, and it was less than a month away. This wasn't just an "Oh crap, it would've been cool to fight in Vegas" type of thing. It also meant that I wasn't going to get paid that month. Without thinking, I took to Twitter and tweeted, "Hey (Jones), you can send my rent check to PO Box 198, NJ." I then went to grab some lunch with my training partners and hash out what had just happened. On the way to eat, my training partner/friend Jeff informed me that my tweet had been retweeted something like 700 times already. That was insane. Nothing I had ever posted before had been retweeted more than 50 times. I'm not going to lie, my first thought was, "Whoops, I hope this doesn't get me in trouble."

> **Without thinking, I took to Twitter with, "Hey (Jones), you can send my rent check to PO Box 198, NJ."**

See, social media is a double-edged sword. People can love and resonate with what you say, or they can absolutely turn against you and turn you into an example. Well, people were resonating with my tweet, and it continued to be retweeted over 2000 times. 90% of the comments I was receiving were supportive, but of course I got some hate as well. "You can't even support your family! ... Quit fighting and get a job! ... You suck!" Of course, I could support my family

(Amanda works too). My words were said in jest. So, as the story continued to evolve, my tweet was continuing to gain speed. It had been posted on some of the most relevant MMA related websites and Twitter accounts. It culminated that weekend when Mike called me and exclaimed, "My dad just saw your tweet on ESPN! Watch the next episode of SportsCenter!" And, 30 minutes later, I saw my name, face and Twitter handle (@SpaniardMMA) up on the screen during SportsCenter with the analyst quoting my name and words. My immediate thought was "Jon Jones doesn't even know my name, and I'm sure he isn't seeing any of this. Right?!" At the time, he was dealing with an onslaught of media issues, so I figured I'd slide under the radar. Not so much.

Fast-forward a month, and we were both on site at UFC 152 in Toronto. After some shuffling, Jon and I were both rescheduled to fight on the same card, a month after the botched Vegas card. Mike, Chris Wing (my other cornerman) and I were taking bets on whether or not anything would come of this entire situation ... when Jon and I came face-to-face. This is how it went down: I had arrived at the UFC office in the Toronto hotel and was checking in. In my mind, I was convinced the issue had passed and was dead in the water. Within minutes of my arrival, Jon entered into the room and bee-lined it straight for me. How he knew I was there, I have no idea. I've heard rumors that someone tipped him off but can't confirm that. "If you have something to say to me, as a man," he said, "say it to my face." Many things were running through my mind. Initially I thought, "Okay, this is like the toughest man in the world, and he is angry at me, confronting me. He's about 35 pounds heavier than me and his wrestling is as good as or better than mine. We are at a UFC event, so there is no way he will actually cross that line and turn this physical. And if he does, I'll probably get a lot of money." We proceeded to have some words, and at the end of it, and we basically agreed to disagree. I don't, and never did, harbor any actual negative feelings toward him. He is the best in the world. None of us has any idea what it is like to make a decision in his shoes. I was simply expressing my frustration. So as this was happening (Mike and Chris might tell you differently), my memory is as follows: Jon and I were face-to-face, and Mike and Chris were basically behind me, maybe off to the side a little. My recollection is of them standing on eggshells, a bit in awe and amazement, and a bit in the realization that this might go south. I think we'd all agree on that part. (Mike is well-trained and has a background in being a bodyguard, and Chris is a professional fighter as well). As soon as Jon left, I looked at them and said, "Okay, how did I do?!" It was like they went from total awe and shock to "Man, he totally owned you! I'd give you a C, maybe C+ on that one," as if I were such a wuss for the way I acted! I still laugh when I think about it. On the other side of almost getting in a fight with one of the toughest men on earth, my friends were now in the driver seat to tell me what I SHOULD have done. What an experience.

THE HATE

When I started my career in MMA, I wasn't involved in social media. My friends (Jack Zerby and Matt Anderson) gave me a lot of their time in creating my website. And, as my career grew, so did my presence online. It's important as a fighter, or as any public figure, to capture as big an audience as possible to build a following of fans, and the majority of this experience is positive. One thing I was not prepared for, though, was the haters. The people who sit at home and go out of their way to sling hate your way or to gather as many people as possible to jointly sling hate your way. I guess to people already in the public eye, this is an obvious part of the game. But for me, it was new and awful. It took me virtually my entire career before I genuinely stopped caring. It was incredible to me that someone would sit at home and message me hateful comments (about me personally, my fighting ability, my family, you name it) without any sort of provoking. And then, when you block them from commenting on your media page, they create another name and continue their rant against you. When I got knocked out against Castillo, you would have thought I went on national TV and kicked all of the puppies in the world at the same time. They hated me! I had one person who sent me nine pages of Twitter comments (9 pages x 140 characters per page=

One thing I was not prepared for, though, was the haters.

1260 characters) telling me the most hateful things you could imagine. I was lying on my couch, having just suffered a concussion, wallowing in the hate. I responded to this "person," and they immediately reversed their position and started sending supportive, encouraging messages. It was at this moment that I realized I needed to stop caring. It was negative energy. These people are faceless cowards.

Unfortunately, not all of the hate is from miscellaneous online sources. There are people close to home whose lifelong goal is to bring me down. To be honest, I'm not sure why. All I do is what I do. I've had countless people try to sabotage me (again, I'm not actually sure what they are sabotaging) for no reason. People who orchestrate other mindless people to slander me at any chance they get. In no way am I suggesting that I am the only one who receives this hatred because it exists at every level. And the only real way to handle it is to pay it no mind. I relate it to arguing with a child. They don't yet know how to properly behave and carry themselves. These haters don't either. So, when you engage with them and try to talk rationally, you are essentially talking with a child. I am not perfect and don't claim to be. I simply carry on every day being the best version of me that I can be. So, if it's your goal to raise your own morale by bringing down me or anyone else, remember this quote: "You know it's time for self-reflection when you're strongly irritated with the successes of others." To those putting themselves out there and striving to succeed, don't take it personally. Here's another quote: "Behind every successful person is a crowd full of haters." I'm right there beside you.

Fortunately, the love and support I have received during my career far outweighs any negativity I have encountered. I get more and more meaningful messages than I could count. Messages that let me know my journey is inspiring, that I serve as a good role model for children, things I don't think of on a daily basis. As I said, I just "be" me. So thank you all for the positive encouragement over the years. I have saved and reread many of the messages.

FIGHT'S OFF, SORRY

One of the most difficult things to endure as a mixed martial artist is the instability of the sport. And, when I say instability, I mean in almost every way. Fighters are fickle, promoters can be fickle, money in general is not plentiful, and therefore people are always hustling in one way or another. Fights often get cancelled with very short notice. I've had several fights fall through at the last second (and believe me, anyone who has fought has most likely endured this as well). A few cancelled fights stick out in my memory. I was scheduled to fight near East Stroudsburg, PA, and I had sold close to 100 tickets to the event. The more tickets you sell, the more money you make. After weigh-ins and the prefight physical examination, we were on the road to my apartment to relax for the day. The fight was later that night. While on the road, I received a call from the promoter saying that my opponent had failed his eye exam, and the fight was off. There was nothing we could do. This was terrible for many reasons. I had trained my butt off to fight, and now it was not happening. I was not going to get paid (though it turned out that I did receive a good portion of my purse). Imagine working for a month and then on payday your boss says, "Sorry, can't pay you for that last month of work." I had to call the 100 people to whom I had sold tickets and tell them that I wouldn't be fighting. Many of them would now not be attending the show, which means I had to retrieve their money from the promoter, which means my income would most likely decrease again. It was overwhelming to say the least. Thankfully, I had my best team with me, my family. We spent the rest of the day making phone calls and returning money.

Fight cancellations are just part of the game. With a sport that is so fickle, and at the same time dangerous, you have to go with the flow. As MMA continues to grow and evolve I am sure that protocol will be put into place to help avoid these instances. I've been on the receiving end of the bad news, but I've also benefitted from guys dropping out of their fights at the last minute (for instance, the Rick Story fight). In the fast-moving world of MMA, it pays to be ready at all times.

THE SPANIARD T-SHIRTS

My first real introduction into MMA, as in world class MMA, was through Eddie Alvarez, who I have mentioned a few times. Eddie came to a gym in my hometown to give a seminar many years ago, and I naturally picked his brain about everything. One of the first things I picked up is that he is a master at self–promotion. Through his own ups and downs, Eddie learned the value of promoting himself to maximize every aspect of his career—more exposure, more ticket sales, more money. This lesson is the most valuable piece of advice I've taken from him, and one of the most important pieces of advice I've received in my entire career. One of the slogans I've lived by—fought by—is "If I don't go around promoting myself, who else will?"

One of the slogans I've lived by is "If I don't go around promoting myself, who else will?"

If you teach me, I will follow your path. The fall of 2007 found me fighting at the Tropicana in Atlantic City, New Jersey. This was the first real test of my career, and to be honest, I was pretty sure I was in over my head. But I was going to do it, and I was going to do it with a bang. Atlantic City is a five-hour trip from Hollidaysburg, and even this early in my career, I had a very loyal fan base. Many of them were prepared to make the trip to Atlantic City. So taking what I learned from Eddie, the "Spaniard T-shirt" was born. What started out as a simple royal blue shirt sporting my family crest turned into an entity of its own.

When I began fighting professionally in 2007, it was clear from the beginning that we (my team, family, and fans) were going to learn on the fly. MMA was so far out of our reality at that time, that we just kind of embraced its newness. And, as I began to expose myself to new and different experiences within the sport, I began taking notes. I was entering this sport to be the best, and I wanted to do everything possible to place the odds in my favor.

I was very green to MMA when Eddie came to my gym to do a seminar. I listened attentively to every word that he spoke. Most of the words pertained to MMA techniques, but he also spoke about self-promotion. Prior to that point, I had never thought of the word "promotion", let alone "self-promotion." What Eddie said that day has stuck with me for the better part of a decade, and it spawned the creation of the "Spaniard T-shirts." With his invaluable knowledge that only comes from experience, I set out on a path that would differentiate me from the pack.

With each fight and new location, there was an opportunity to create something special, an original t–shirt for my family, friends, and fans to show their support. It became a "thing" for my fans to ask which shirt they should wear to certain fights, so that everyone could be coordinated in showing their support. The very first design, "Family Crest", created a buzz in the Tropicana Casino in Atlantic City that lasted close to a decade. The t–shirts were created through the hard work of just a few people—largely Matt Anderson (friend and designer) and my brother Ben. We were also fortunate to build relationships with some very good local businesses in and around Hollidaysburg, my hometown. The Locker Room and RC's Print Specialists were always up for helping out in any way to help create/print the t–shirts in time for competition.

We have created more than ten "Spaniard T-shirts", but each one of them has maintained a common theme. I am extremely proud of who I am and where I come from, so we always included local pride whenever possible. We also developed themes—color schemes, landmarks, designs, etc.—that were pertinent to the location of the fight. One of my favorite shirts is the "Black and Gold", which proudly shows off the Steelers' colors; it was part of the biggest night in my professional career (victory over Rick Story), as my fans sported "Black and Gold" throughout the Consol Energy Center.

As I've mentioned a few times in the book, Sheetz has been a strong supporter of mine throughout my career. What started out as a small, local convenience store has blossomed into an entity of its own on the east coast. For several years now, Sheetz has sponsored my "walkout shirt", the shirt I wear to the cage. As a team, we developed two special designs, incorporating both their original and newer, updated logos.

I want to send out a big, personal "Thank You" to anyone and everyone who played a role in the "Spaniard T-shirt." Whether you were a fan showing your support, helped design it, or aided in their production, THANK YOU!

The following pages contain Spaniard T-shirt designs that we have specifically created for various events throughout my career.

Family Crest
Fan Shirt, 2007

WWW.CHARLIE-BRENNEMAN.COM

Spaniard Nation
Fan Shirt, 2008

TROOPS

www.Charlie-Brenneman.com

FORT HOOD, TX

UFC UFN 23, Fight for the Troops — Fort Hood, TX
Fan Shirt, January 22, 2011

UFC Live 4 – Pittsburgh, PA
Walkout Shirt, June 26, 2011

SPANIARD

UFC Live 4 — Pittsburgh, PA
Fan Shirt, June 26, 2011

UFC Live 6 – Washington, DC
Fan Shirt, October 1, 2011

UFC on FX – Nashville, TN
Fan Shirt, January 20, 2012

UFC on FX 3 – Fort Lauderdale, FL
Fan Shirt, June 8, 2012

UFC 152 – Toronto, CAN
(Though designed for UFC 151 – Las Vegas. NV)

Fan Shirt, September 22, 2012

VFL 40 – Altoona, PA

Fan Shirt, January 19, 2013

CFFC 28 – Atlantic City, NJ
(Though designed for CFFC 26 – Atlantic City, NJ)

Walkout Shirt, October 26, 2013

UFC 172 – Baltimore, MD
Fan Shirt, April 26, 2014

MESSAGE FROM "THE SPANIARD"

I want to thank every one of you for taking the time to read my book. Family, friends and fans have fueled my career (and life), and I am especially grateful for each one of you. As I continue to evolve and share my message, I encourage you all to stay current on my latest endeavors via the Internet and social media.

You can find me at:

Web	charlie-brenneman.com
Facebook	Charlie "The Spaniard" Brenneman
Twitter	@SpaniardMMA
Instagram	MMASpaniard
Snapchat	SpaniardMMA

ABOUT THE AUTHOR

Charlie "The Spaniard" Brenneman is a professional mixed martial arts fighter, speaker and mentor. Following a successful high school wrestling career, Charlie took his talents to Lock Haven University where he achieved a top 12 finish at Division I Nationals and 1st Team All-Academic. After teaching Spanish for three years and winning Spike TV's *Pros vs. Joes,* Charlie decided to leave his job to pursue a master's degree and begin his professional fighting career—"The Spaniard" was born. In 2011, he was ranked as high as #7 in the world. "The Spaniard" has fought at the highest level of the sport in three countries. He currently lives in PA with his wife and daughter.

Made in the USA
Middletown, DE
07 November 2015